Our age is a time of change in the universe and earth, a time of increasing awareness of the connectedness of peoples and cultures, of male and female, a time of reconnecting with our whole selves. Arising with and from the great movements of our time — Civil Rights, the Women's Movement, Gay Rights, Anti-War — is an increasing return to and recognition of the Goddess and of women's spirituality. *The Kwan Yin Book of Changes* is a reclaiming of the ancient Chinese *I Ching* that returns her wisdoms to the feminine and to the Goddess.

The Kwan Yin Book of Changes places the ancient Chinese *I Ching*, a divinatory system much a complement to the tarot, in a context that women and men in touch with peace can relate to. The patriarchalism and rigidity of the traditional *I Ching* is exchanged for a women-only communal government and world, with situations and language relevant to modern occult women and to men who relate to the feminine aspects of themselves. The God/Emperor of traditional translations is replaced by the immanence of the earth and the Goddess, and fate and predestiny give way to free will and choice. The Superior Man of the old versions is the Superior or Spiritual Woman in a system much more positive than any earlier *I Ching* translation.

Unique in fields of women's studies, *I Ching* studies, Hopi religion, philosophy, tarot and women's spirituality and wicca, *The Kwan Yin Book of Changes* is a new aspect of the return to women's spirituality. A formerly all-male divinatory tool is made relevant once again to women, its patriarchal obscuring of women's power returned. Women who purchase and appreciate books by Starhawk, Vicki Noble, Z. Budapest, Gail Fairfield, Marion Weinstein, Margot Adler, *et. al.* will find much to interest them in *The Kwan Yin Book of Changes*. The book involves the studies of *I Ching*, wicca, the Chinese Calendar, the zodiac, Native American religion, and the tarot, connecting and relating these studies, and involving all of them in the feminine reclaiming of the Great Goddess and of women's worlds.

As a divinatory tool, *The Kwan Yin Book of Changes* returns the Chinese *I Ching* to women's use, and is a tool of great power simple to use. The book stands the *I Ching* side by side with the tarot as an aspect of women's spirituality, and is a re-membering of the submerged skills of women's matriarchy and culture.

About Diane Stein

Diane Stein is the author of *The Goddess Book of Days, The Women's Book of Healing, The Women's Spirituality Book,* and *The Kwan Yin Book of Changes,* as well as of several tapes. Involved with the women's movement and women's spirituality almost from their beginnings, she is a healer, psychic, witch and priestess of the Goddess craft, and a writer whose work has been known to women since 1969. An activist in the women's, gay rights, disability rights, and anti-war movements, her work has focused on inter-relating them with women's spirituality and on using her quests for knowledge and inter-relatedness to teach.

Diane Stein was born on September 22, 1948 and holds an MA in English Literature from the University of Pittsburgh, and a BS degree in Education and English from Duquesne University.

About Vicki Noble

Vicki Noble is co-creator (with Karen Vogel) of the round *Motherpeace Tarot Deck,* and author of *Motherpeace: A Way to the Goddess Through Myth, Art and Tarot.* She is an artist, activist, teacher and healer who lives in Arizona.

To Write to the Author

We cannot guarantee that every letter written to the author can be answered, but all will be forwarded. Both the author and the publisher appreciate hearing from readers, learning of your enjoyment and benefit from this book. Llewellyn also publishes a bi-monthly news magazine with news and reviews of practical esoteric studies and articles helpful to the student, and some readers' questions and comments to the author may be answered through this magazine's columns if permission to do is included in the original letter. The author sometimes participates in seminars and workshops, and dates and places are announced in *The Llewellyn New Times.* To write to the author, or to ask a question, write to:

Diane Stein
c/o THE LLEWELLYN NEW TIMES
P.O. Box 64383-760, St. Paul, MN 55164-0383, U.S.A.

Please enclose a self-addressed, stamped envelope for reply, or $1.00 to cover costs.

ABOUT THE KWAN YIN BOOK OF CHANGES

The Kwan Yin Book of Changes translates the male-dominated Chinese *I Ching* to women's values and into a Goddess system of religion. Where the traditional *I Ching* operates on a basis of destiny and resignation, *The Kwan Yin Book of Changes* is rooted instead in action and free choice within the cosmos of natural law. The supreme being is the earth, the Goddess and Mother. Where the traditional *I Ching* bases earthly government on the emperor and his hierarchy of servitors, *The Kwan Yin Book of Changes* is a matriarchal government ruled by the consensus of the women who comprise her and where every woman within her is a ruler. Since each woman has a direct role in governing, and since each woman has a skill or skills she can offer, there are no Inferior vs. Superior persons. The woman of matriarchy, at whatever level, is the Superior Woman. The women of matriarchy take on various roles, and each woman may be any or all of the roles of Mother, Priestess, Daughter, Sister, Wisewoman. There are no men at all to dominate or co-opt. Each woman nurtures and is nurtured, teaches and is taught, gives and receives in her growing and maturing of skills. All women are equally Superior Women. All women rule, and the matriarchy benefits from each woman's contributions to her. Spirituality, divinity and natural law are Goddess-based, with connections made to the zodiac, the wiccan calendar, the Hopi Road of Life, and the tarot (*Motherpeace* and *Choice-Centered* philosophies). The Spiritual and Superior Woman is connected to the Wheel of Life and Change, to the order and harmony of the universe.

Personal relationships, the emphasis on most of Part II of the *I Ching*, is rooted in *The Kwan Yin Book of Changes* on the relationship between two women. Mother to Daughter, Sister to Sister, and lover to lover are the basic relationships within matriarchy. The Mother is a woman who teaches and leads in the running of the community by her skills at interactions and mediation. The Priestess leads spiritually, connecting women to the Goddess in their everyday lives. The Daughter is someone who learns — not necessarily as a child, but she is also the child. The Wisewoman is the sage and healer who has withdrawn from the community to the quiet of interior learning. Sisters are each and every woman of matriarchy. Lovers are the relationships between two women who choose to share their lives and to care for each other, to live together as a family.

The traditional and *Kwan Yin I Chings* are composed of 64 hexagrams, and are strong divinatory tools, but *The Kwan Yin Book of Changes* diverges often totally from traditional titles and hexagram texts. Hexagram 54, *The Marrying Maiden*, for example in Wilhelm-Baynes, is *Living Together* in this matriarchal version. Defeatist and sexist philosophies are changed to action choices and feminist awareness. The Superior Woman controls her life and directs her destiny, and she is each and all of us.

A modern women's reclaiming of the Chinese *Book of Changes* is long overdue. Coming from a civilization where the woman warrior is still very much alive in tradition and legend, the *I Ching* as we have known it has been patriarchally obscured. *The Kwan Yin Book of Changes* is an attempt to change this. She is a new cornerstone in women's reclaiming of spirituality and the Goddess.

Other Books by Diane Stein

The Kwan Yin Book of Changes
    Llewellyn Publications, 1985
The Women's Spirituality Book
    Llewellyn Publications, 1986
The Women's Book of Healing
    Llewellyn Publications, 1988
Innocence/experience, short fiction
    Woman Prints, 1981
Stroking the Python: Women's Psychic Experiences
    Llewellyn Publications, 1988

Tapes

Rachida Finds Magick
    Llewellyn Publications, 1986
Two Meditations: The Goddess Within/The Rainbow,
    Llewellyn Publications, 1986
The Kwan Yin Workshop Tape
    Llewellyn Publications, 1986
The Crystal Healing Workshop Tape,
    Llewellyn Publications, 1986

Forthcoming:
    A Book of Women's Rituals
    The Women's Book of Healing, Volume Two

THE
KWAN YIN

(Goddess of Mercy and Knowledge)

BOOK OF CHANGES

The ancient *I Ching*, Book of Life, is adapted to invoke the aid and blessings of the Feminine Principle in answering the questions and needs of women, and men, today.

By
DIANE STEIN

Foreword by Vicki Noble

1993
Llewellyn Publications
St. Paul, Minnesota 55164-0383, U.S.A.

FIRST EDITION, 1985
Fifth Printing, 1993

Cover image by Katlyn Miller
Book design by Terry Buske
Illustrations by Robin Wood

Library of Congress Cataloging-in-Publication Data
Stein, Diane, 1948-
   The Kwan Yin book of changes.

   Adaption of: I Ching
   Bibliography: p.
   1. Divination—China. 2. I ching. 3. Goddesses—China.
4. Women and religion—China. I. I ching. English. II. Title.
BF1773.2.C5S86   1985   133.3′3   85-45287
ISBN 0-87542-760-X

Llewellyn Publications
A Division of Llewellyn Worldwide, Ltd.
P.O. 64383, St. Paul, MN 55164-0383

for brenwyn

TABLE OF CONTENTS

preface

In ancient predynastic China, women were the healers or shamans, the practitioners of magic and divination, who were called "Wu" and came from the South. Chinese scholar Joseph Needham describes the Wu as women who danced and wore feathers in imitation of birds, like so many shamans in other parts of the world. The ancient Chinese oracle bone symbol for Wu (meaning "to heal") looks like figure A. It was later modified and "modernized" to the current character for "wu" which looks like figure B. This abstraction of what was once pictographic corresponds to the gradual and complete replacement in Chinese culture of the Wu by men who took over the arts of healing. By the time of the Han dynasty, we read that the Wu were no longer allowed in the courts.

figure A   figure B

The ancient Chinese Book of Changes (called the *I Ching*) is a body of knowledge or wisdom contained in oracular form which allows for "divination" or the practice of divining the character of a present or future situation. It is one of the oldest written documents in the world and has its roots in the pre-patriarchal world of ancient China and the Wu. However, it has not come down through the ages untouched. It was written down only after the advent of patriarchal dynastic power in China (already changing its basic nature), and it has gone through major modifications since then, including even the complete reversal of meaning given to the basic two elements, "yin" (female) and "yang" (male). The modern "authorized" version most familiar to western readers is the Wilhelm/Baynes translation.

Diane Stein's *The Kwan Yin Book of Changes* is modeled after the traditional structure, so it will be familiar to students and regular practitioners of the oracle. Unlike many modern interpretations, Stein has not made this book a literal "how to" manual of advice and consultation. Rather, the hexagrams contain their original inscrutability, reading like images caught in a pool of water or on a steamy glass window in winter. You catch your reflection or a glimpse of your situation through the "readings", and this glimmer of truth resonates with your deeper knowledge, bringing meaning to your situation. In this way, the hexagrams are meditations or koans.

Stein's major revision is the reclaiming of the feminine, or content of the ancient work and the removal of all patriarchal language and imagery. In this version you will find no Army, no superior Man, and no masculine creative principle. Stein herself envisions an all-female world, a "matriarchal society" in which women are both governors and the governed. It is not necessary, however, to be a separatist from men in order to benefit from and enjoy her book. I use it as an imaginary all-female inner space where it is possible to "try on" every role without having to stretch into the usual patriarchal or masculinist forms. This total female inclusion is possible in no other version of the *I Ching* and is a very healing experience for women.

Men too will be drawn to this version of the *I Ching*. When Karen Vogel and I first made the *Motherpeace Tarot Cards*, we wondered if they would turn out to be for "women only". On the contrary, they are quite useful to men who are opening to the feminine aspects of themselves, as well as to the powerful aspects of the women in their lives. For years I have hoped for a "women's *I Ching*" that would update and revise the ancient words of wisdom to the point where men and women reading it could not automatically assume masculine-yang-good, feminine-yin-bad, the way that the old versions are inclined to do.

When I first received this manuscript in the mail, I asked the traditional *I Ching* (Wilhelm/Baynes version) what "it" thought of Diane Stein's new work. My throw of the coins came up all yin, the number Two hexagram, called Kun, "the Receptive". Both Wilhelm/Baynes and

Stein speak of Kun as the earth, the female-maternal, the state of Nature and manifestation. But the Wilhelm/Baynes book insists that only when the Feminine is responding to the Creative (masculine) is it good; when it "abandons this position and tries to stand as an equal side by side with the Creative, does it become evil". This kind of obvious social commentary (probably added by Confucians much later than the original material) is naturally deleted from Stein's framework which acknowledges the true equality and partnership between the two basic elements.

Because Stein's *I Ching* is the first feminist version of this ancient Book, I believe it will be received with pleasure by men and women interested in breaking from traditional sex-role stereotypes and moving toward personal integrity. The hexagrams are beautifully written, and their counsel is useful to the heart.

Vicki Noble
Winter Solstice 1984

foreword

For thousands of years and planetwide, women's pride and spirituality have been submerged beneath the dominance of patriarchal forces. From families to jobs to governments to religious practices, women's culture has been repressed, the female principle in both men and women obscured and excluded by systems too frightened to accept their power. The result has been decay and dehumanization, the threat of nuclear war, disconnection from nature and the Wheel of Life, overpopulation and overpoverty, and a serious loss and waste of psychic and healing skill. The oppression and denial of the life force, the repression of women, and the submergence of the female self that exists in all are universal, but today's approaching Age of Aquarius has begun to reconnect the Wheel. Women are reasserting their life power, and men are finding that power within them. Women's spirituality is rebalancing and healing the earth for the benefit of male and female alike.

The Great Goddess, the creative power of the female principle, has never left us. There have always been Daughters and Mothers, Priestesses, lovers, Wisewomen, and witches of both sexes despite the incredible persecutions of patriarchy. The Great Mother's mysteries and knowledge have not been destroyed, but much is lost to us and more has gone underground. The Goddess' re-emergence, the return of the oneness of all life and the female principle in men and women has begun a new awareness and a new time. Women and new men everywhere are dis-covering and re-membering (Mary Daly terms) the Goddess, denying her oppressors and reviving her rituals, values and lifestyles. Through the last great spasms of the Age of Pisces, through the violences of war, rape, moral majorities, and female infanticide in India and China, the Goddess is emerging again. The new age is reclaiming female power, the female life principle, and ending the fragmenting forces of death and lovelessness that have kept our world in chains.

In the beginning was the Goddess who birthed the universe, the many Goddesses of the east and west, of Africa, the Orient, Egypt, South America and Europe. There were Yemaya, Kwan Yin and Amaterasu, Pele, Isis and Astarte, Shekinah, Changing Woman, Brigid and Demeter. Whatever she was called by her worshippers, the Great Mother reigned, and the earth was respected as her body and her home. The Goddess was loved by men and women both; she was not feared as gods are feared, for she was both creator and participant, mother and oneself, the female and male of all that lives. Women were her mirrors, her own image, and were part of her; men respected and worshipped her as her created opposites and as part of her, as well. The Goddess was the equal giver and taker of life, the changer from infancy to strength to old age. She was the Wheel of birth, death and rebirth, the Wheel of the turning seasons, of the interconnectedness of the earth, the universe and humanity.

In women is the Goddess' mystery, the secret of birth and creation that men share but cannot duplicate. In every woman also lies the male principle, as in every male is the Goddess. Yet while men and women are both born, only women bleed monthly and birth new lives from their bodies as the Goddess birthed the universe. They reproduce not only themselves but men as well, and nurture both from their breasts. Envied and feared by some cultures' men in early days, women's place in society reflected their culture's reverence or nonreverence of birth. Where women were seen as part of the world-birthing Goddess, they were priestesses, rulers, mothers, healers and sages — they participated in a dominance or partnership with men. Where women were seen as afterthoughts, made and not born by a male god from a male rib, women were restricted to mothering and sex, to being 'the other' whose power had to be carefully segregated and controlled. In Goddess worshipping societies that were mostly matriarchal, women were the initiators of community, farming and agriculture, basketry, weaving and pottery making, the domestication of animals — of civilization. In these societies, men and women were opposites, but in an interconnected balance. In patriarchies that came later, these same creative women were denied humanity, denied opportunity, contribution, choices and education, and prevented by law or custom from independent lives.

The split of creation from birth began when men discovered their part in reproduction. They attempted to control birth by controlling women, by separating the female principle from both men and from the Goddess and instituting male gods. From women and men as part of the Goddess, only men became and remained gods, and women and children were bound to them. By the force of patriarchy, rape and incest began, as men who could not duplicate birth devalued it and tried to own it. Gods that elevated the male were brought to power, gods that had no birth origins, and the Goddess was suppressed with increasing severity. The female principle, the value of birth and the all-partaking life force, was fragmented and submerged.

But women's mysteries did not end with patriarchal denial. Despite increasing restrictions, goddess worship continued to be practiced by women and some men. The new religions that separated creation from birth compounded their losses by separating earth from the universe. From the harmony of beginnings, endings, and new beginnings in natural cycles — the Wheel and oneness of life — nonfemale religions offered guilt and suffering on earth for the reward of salvation later in heaven. The few saved were usually male, and individual men were installed as intercessors between earth and god. The female principle in men was lost, and women were rigidly and ruthlessly suppressed. As late as three hundred years ago, nine million people were burned at the stake to enforce this split. Most of them were women who refused to let go of the Goddess, women and men who retained forbidden skills as witches, healers, midwives and psychics in the Goddess tradition. Even through this period, the female principle — an intrinsic part of male and female — remained. The powers of women's spirituality, of the long repressed mother Goddess, still refused to die.

Women today, and a few aware men, are beginning to reaffirm the Goddess religion, the earth, and their own connectedness with all life. Their increasing creativity and initiative, their strength, positivity and responsibility, is reflected in personal achievements and in various unifying social movements. The growing consciousness of the civil rights, gay rights, and women's movements is becoming global, along with gaining awareness and activism on issues of nuclear power, anti-war work, environmentalism, anti-racism, hunger, disability rights and freedom of choice. All life is interconnected and the earth is a part of ourselves.

This is not to say that the thousands of years' entrenchment of patriarchy is over. The Goddess worshipper's freedom to "Do what you will harming none" exists for few men anywhere and for certainly fewer women. As long as men have dominated, women's culture, artists, writers, musicians, philosophers and leaders have been rigidly denied and repressed. Heroic efforts are being made by today's women to locate, document and make known the creative achievements and art of women of the past, and heroic efforts are still needed to recognize, value, nurture and preserve the work of women now living. In all facets of modern life, women are denied choices, denied acknowledgement, denied respect, and often denied survival. This is even more tragically true for women of color than for white women, for lesbians than for heterosixual women, for women in nonwestern countries and for disabled women everywhere. Too much has been lost under thousands of years of patriarchy, but gains begin to be made.

The women's spirituality movement, the resurgence of the Great Goddess and the female principle, is one of the outgrowths of the Second Wave women's movement since 1969. Along with insistence by women on equality in law and earning power, in educational, artistic and other opportunity, is the seeking for a women's religion. Patriarchal religions, with their societies' denigration and exclusion of women and the female in men, have lost acceptance in women's and men's lives. Traditional Christianity's "Dominate the earth" attitude and the Jewish and Islamic's "Thank god I was not born a woman" hold decreasing persuasion, despite many women's and men's work to revitalize and change them. There has been the new re-membrance of a women's religion, a religion that values all life, and through thousands of years of repression it still exists. Women today are discovering and reclaiming this religion, as they dis-cover and reclaim themselves.

The Great Goddess was not eradicated under patriarchy, but was submerged, co-opted and transformed. The Judaic Lilith, the first woman before Eve, became a goblin to frighten children with, and the Shekinah, the female polarity of Yahweh, was almost fully repressed. The Christian Mary, a borrowed Goddess, became so popular in the Middle Ages that the Church made vigorous campaigns to lessen her power. Christian holy days were set at wiccan sabbats and replaced them, since the sabbats were attended by whole communities and couldn't be wiped out. In the Greek Hera, a twisted vestige of the

Great Mother is seen, transformed thanklessly to a nagging wife of the god, and temple priestesses were degraded as prostitutes in Rome and India. More recently, American Indian, African and Polynesian cultures and god-and-goddess cycles were destroyed under slavery, or by missionaries in their own homes. As in the rest of women's culture, much is lost beyond redemption, but much is being regained.

A return to Goddess worship means a reaffirmation of creativity and birth, the female principle in men and women, and the interconnectedness in life. The Goddess is both the earth and the heavens. She is all that lives, and all that lives is part of her. To pollute the earth by nuclear leakage, therefore, is to pollute the Goddess and oneself. To deal in the oppression of any gender or minority is to disrespect the Goddess. To cause harm brings harm in return.

There is no guilt in women's spirituality, only free will and responsibility. Power that comes from within, from being part of the creation-birthing Goddess, brings choices and consequences instead of blame. Joy is intrinsic and money is not evil — good or evil lies only in how the resources are gained and used. Sexuality is both responsibility and joy, while rape and pornography are not sexuality but assault. Protection from harm lies in free will, for both harmful and good acts return to the doer. There is gentleness in men and strength in women, since men and women are equal beings, and youth, adulthood and old age are equal parts of the Wheel.

In the female spirituality principle, a woman or man controls by choice the course of her life and lives it now; she is not bound by predestiny or released by heaven later. Most Goddess worshippers believe in reincarnation and generation after death. Life extends beyond the body, and one's energy and Daughters remain after them.

Life in the Goddess religion is a Wheel of birth to death changes that reflect the changes of the earth. In an all female telling, the Goddess as Daughter awakens at Brigid (February 2) in the snow, and proceeds to grow with the birthing and awakening spring. She finds joyful passion at Beltane in May, and passes from Daughter to pregnant Mother at the Summer Solstice. As Mother she births the harvest of the year, first fruits at Lammas (August 1) and the gathering-in at the Fall Equinox (September 22). She becomes the aging Wisewoman in the waning year, bringing death and passing into it on Hallows Eve (October 31) until her rebirth at the Winter Solstice (December 22). The Wheel of the Year begins again with Brigid, and repeats.

In Goddess traditions that incorporate the god, a balancing male consort shares the cycles. In this case, the Daughter Goddess awakens at Brigid with the infant god. They play together with the Spring Equinox (March 22), the rebirthing year, and find growth and sexuality at Beltane (May 1). Their love consummated at the June 21 Summer Solstice, the god dies to become the seed of harvest, and the mourning Goddess becomes Wisewoman and Harvester. She gives birth to him again at Winter Solstice, becoming new herself. There are endless variations of both versions of the Year.

Women's mysteries today seek to re-enact and re-member the birth to death phases of the year and lunar cycles. The Wheel itself remains to us, but much of the tradition and diversity of world Goddess cultures has been lost or obscured. Reclaiming the Goddess and the female principle of humanity means not only reclaiming her rituals, but redesigning, reinventing, reinterpreting and reweaving (another Mary Daly term) these rituals in light of modern life. Along with dis-covering the Goddess' legends of the world and re-enacting her Wheel of the Year, women and wiccan men work to relearn lost healing, psychic and personal power skills. Knowledge of herbs, midwifery, homeopathy, meditation, aura and crystal healing, empathy and telepathy are part of the female principle of creating life and are only limited to women by the patriarchal separation of earth from universe. Reaffirming these skills and relearning the Tarot, *I Ching* and other psychic tools is an Age of Aquarius task. Their re-membering brings women's power and culture back from under thousands of years' repression, and offers it to both women and men. Where women regain these forces in themselves and men regain their female aspects through them, the goal is reached, and the life force is named and sustained for all.

The Kwan Yin Book of Changes is an act of reclaiming and re-birthing the Goddess and the female principle. Like other wisdoms lost or nearly so under patriarchy, the female has been removed from traditional existing *I Ching* versions. Only a misogynist remnant, though a powerful one, has remained of what the original must have been. The work's very one-sidedness and denial of the female principle indicates the suppression of earlier women's roots. By developing a Goddess' *I Ching*, reweaving and re-membering its creative balance on the Wheel of Life, several things occur.

First of all, women's involvement and power are dis-covered in a valuable psychic skill. The patriarchal *I Ching* has written women out, and therefore, dis-attracted them from using it, but the tool itself has much to offer. The *I Ching* is a strong form of wisdom and divination, with great similarities to the also reclaimed Tarot. It appeals to an audience often broader than Tarot, when women are not excluded from it, because the *I Ching* is a written work in a verbal society. The book offers in-depth readings in less time than a Tarot reading involves, and requires less skill initially to use. Its media of the printed page has limitless creative possibilities, including that of returning its wisdoms to women.

The Kwan Yin Book of Changes is also a meditation cycle and a Wheel of the Goddess Year. Passages drawn in readings extend to meditation tools that lead further into the divination process. The Wheel of the Year is a fully perfected meditation tool itself, and coupling it with written passages increases it. Like other learnings, too traditional meditation techniques have excluded women to the point where women cannot use them, and *The Kwan Yin Book of Changes* is a dis-covering of these techniques, as well.

Another reclaiming in this *I Ching* is the interconnecting of prepatriarchal systems, of women's mysteries that value birth and mirror the oneness of all humanity. Along with its Goddess tradition base and the correspondences made to the Tarot, the book weaves together the zodiac, the ancient Chinese calendar, and the Hopi Road of Life. It re-members some of the lost knowledge of the female principle, and returns women to the days when they were the Priestesses, Mothers, Sisters, Daughters and Wisewomen they are becoming again. The learning of the traditional *I Ching* is made both new and old by being made whole.

While this learning and this *I Ching* are given freely to all who appreciate it, the book is designed and interpreted for women. This is not to deny the Goddess or female principle in men, but to affirm the needs of women for thought that respects and dis-covers what has been lost and taken from them. Through the transition from Goddess worship to patriarchy, through the repressions of Judaism and Christianity, through the burning times and the alienations of modern high technology, women have held tightly and valiantly to the Goddess, to the interconnection of all life. After thousands of years of silence, the Great Mother is being heard again, and women are answering her by re-membering her rituals and knowledge. As part of her knowledge, as a psychic tool, the *I Ching* has withstood centuries of the misogyny illustrated by her footbinding culture. Like women, the Goddess, and the female principle, the *I Ching* has survived, and *The Kwan Yin Book of Changes* is a tribute and reclaiming of that survival. A part of the rising of the world-birthing Goddess, this book is a women's tool.

introduction

Entering the world of the *I Ching*, the world of earth, air, fire and water, of approach and waiting, wisdom and folly, is not immediately comfortable or easy. The rewards for entering, however, of using the *I Ching* for divination, are great. With an attitude of respect for the Mother's wisdoms lent to us, the Chinese *Book of Changes* is very much an element of women's spiritual growth, a knowledge ready for us to reclaim.

Coming from a mystic civilization where the woman as warrior and amazon is still strong in legend, the *I Ching* has been patriarchally obscured. Women have been less drawn to the *I Ching* than to the Tarot, although there are close correspondences between them. Like the Tarot, like women's mysteries, like even schoolbook history (I use the term HIStory advisedly), the *Book of Changes* has roots far deeper than the surface available to women today. As Sally Gearhart's poineering work, *The Feminist Tarot*, earlier revolutionized Tarot studies for women, I hope to bring the *I Ching* back to the women's community with this new edition.

The Kwan Yin Book of Changes is very different from traditional and Chinese versions, in fact is different from the modern versions as well. Where traditional editions and translations are based on a god/ emperor and the rigid caste hierarchy of government officials under him, this *I Ching* is grounded in a Goddess matriarchy. Women within matriarchy are her rulers, by consensus and by their individual abilities. Each woman has her place and is a vital part, and all women within matriarchy are equals of great worth. There are no class, caste, age, wealth or racial issues — all women are one. There are no able

1

and disabled women in matriarchy, for every woman has a skill or skills that are needed. Unlike the Chinese *I Ching* also, there are no inferior and superior participants, for every woman of matriarchy is a Superior Woman.

The Kwan Yin Book of Changes is composed of women only, there are no male principles in her at all, and the male pronoun 'he' or the neutral pronoun 'it' are not employed in the present-tense philosophy or text. The women of matriarchy participate in many roles within her, and every woman is every role. There are the Wisewoman, Priestess, Mother and Daughter, and the Sisters who are all of these.

The Wisewoman is the sage, scholar and healer who chooses to withdraw from the cares of daily matriarchal government. She chooses aloneness as an affirmation. Though she is not active in group decision making, she is welcomed as a vital woman in the community. She is respected and reverenced for what she gives, and respected as well for what she chooses not to share. She is the Crone or Hermit of the Tarot. Nowhere is her age designated or restricted in any way, nor is age specified or restricted in any of the roles.

The next woman of matriarchy is the Priestess, and again she corresponds to a Tarot card, The High Priestess of the major arcana. She is matriarchy's channel and liason to the Goddess, the woman who controls the raising and grounding of spiritual power, and the teacher of Mysteries to all women. She is a role each woman participates in, and each woman who chooses to do so becomes her. The Priestess is matriarchy's connectedness to the Wheel of Life, to the cycles and harmonies of the earth and universe. She leads ritual, and observes and directs the Sabbat and Esbat ceremonies, but even more importantly she connects the women of matriarchy with the spiral of the Goddess in their daily lives.

A Mother in this book may be a woman who bears a child, but she is also a leader in the government of matriarchy. This book is named for her, and for the Mother aspect of the Goddess as well, for without her tact and her skills at organizing and unifying women in groups there would be no matriarchy at all. She is a woman who is clear and connected, who is empathetic and aware. She has the ability to listen, to analyze and soothe — and to take bold and vital action when the time to act arrives. She is The Empress in the Tarot, healing and nurturing. When she rules in matriarchy, she does so by choice of the women around her, and by force of their love. She walks in beauty and she walks in caring. She is the woman who teaches the Daughters, and her Sisters come to her in need.

The Daughter in matriarchy is any woman of any age who comes to another woman to learn, and she is also the Joyous Lake of free potential that is the child. The Daughter of matriarchy is nurtured in a space of safety and of love. She is taught with gentleness by the Mothers of matriarchy and the Priestesses, encouraged to reach out and grow while being protected from harm. In the Tarot, the Daughter is perhaps The Fool of the major arcana, the first innocent beginnings, potential, hope and newness embodied in joy. She is springtime and brightness, the future of matriarchy, perfect trust and flowing love.

Other women in *The Kwan Yin Book of Changes* are the Spiritual Woman and Superior Woman, and they are all of us. The Superior Woman is one who seeks; she is the woman asking questions of the oracle and the one to whom an *I Ching* reading is directed. She is The Significator of the Tarot; she is oneself, the woman of matriarchy. The Spiritual Woman and Superior Woman are interchangeable terms, one applying to the universal and the other to earthly living, just as Part I of the hexagrams are universal and spiritually directed, and Part II are earthly and mundane. The Spiritual and Superior Woman are women who seek deeply. They are Daughter, Mother, Priestess, Wisewoman, Sister, the self and the other, the lover and the loved.

The Superior and Spiritual Woman's Sisters in matriarchy are the women around her. Each Sister is a Superior Woman and a Spiritual Woman; each is all of us in a circle of family and peers. The Sisters are the women who are matriarchy, and who are every role and skill within her. They are women who love each other, love the women around them, and love one special woman as well — and they are also therefore lovers and partners. The Sisters of matriarchy work together, play together, heal and help each other, celebrate together. They share a world and they are the world they share. In couples, they find each special other and they choose to live in harmony, caring and in love. Within matriarchy, the Sisters are fulfilled and safe.

The matriarchy herself, though not a designated individual woman, is all women. She corresponds in *The Kwan Yin Book of Changes* to The World card in the Tarot. She is a community/nation that is the sum of her parts and her parts are the women within her. Ruled by skills given her, each woman of matriarchy lends her strength and learning. She is a consensus based community, grounded in the Wheel of Life and connected to the cycles of the earth. There is struggle in matriarchy at times, but she is faced and resolved. The choices are complex, but the women choose well. They live in unity and peace within the harmonies of nature and the Goddess. The women of matriarchy live together, work together, to make her strong and good, and they succeed.

In the Chinese world view, there is harmony with natural law, but nature is an adversary and life is determined or predetermined by the course of unchangeable fate. In *The Kwan Yin Book of Changes*, these tenets are challenged and revised. The women of matriarchy live as a part of the earth and of all life on her. They are connected to the Wheel of the Year and the Wheel of Life of the Goddess. As a part of the universe too, the Superior Woman is an aspect of the Goddess — she *is* the Goddess, and she is also the earth. The women of matriarchy live at the center of the Wheel and are at one with her. To be in harmony with the cosmos then, is not to submit but to recognize and merge. Correct action by the Superior or Spiritual Woman puts her at one with the universe, and brings her peace and contentment. The Superior Woman, the individual woman, sees herself reflected in the harmony of her Sisters who are the matriarchy with her. Matriarchy is in turn a reflection of the cycles of the Goddess earth, and earth is a mirror of the balanced universe.

The women of matriarchy are not bounded by fate and destiny, but create their own. They take control of their lives by their actions and determine their fates. Through awareness, clarity, connectedness, and caring, the Superior Woman chooses her paths. She takes action when the time is right to act; she waits when she meets a time of waiting; she withdraws in times of withdrawal. But in all things, she is who determines the correctness of the times and the forms of action or decisions she makes. There is the order of natural law in this feminist *I Ching*, but there is also the limitlessness of free will, which is an individual matter. No woman in *The Kwan Yin I Ching* determines another woman's actions or makes her decisions for her. Women help each other, and are there to help each other, but none walks another's paths. Each woman has her place in the Wheel of Life, and she engages in spirituality and learning to understand that place and to learn how to flow with or change her. In the nature of change, women create their own changes; in the nature of endings, women create new beginnings; in the nature of the spiral, women choose their own destinies. No woman affects or influences another's free will without her permission and approval.

Correspondences are made in *The Kwan Yin Book of Changes*

to the Tarot, to the Wiccan Calendar, to the Hopi Road of Life, to the zodiac. Each example of these correspondences is only an example, however, meant to suggest further connections rather than to be definitive. Some hexagrams very obviously connect to Tarot cards (see Appendix II), and a brief and beginning list is given below.

4. Mêng — Youthful Folly	The Fool
8. Pi — Holding Together	The Lovers
15. Chi'en — Temperance	Temperance
24. Fu — The Wheel of Life	The Wheel of Fortune
29. K'an — The Depths	The High Priestess
49. Ko — Change and Transformation	Hanged One
58. Tui — Joy	Ace of Cups

Correspondences become obvious to the user of *The Kwan Yin Book of Changes* who is also aware of the Tarot. In the correspondences to Tarot referenced here, thanks is given to Vicki Noble's exquisite book *Motherpeace: A Way to the Goddess Through Myth, Art and Tarot*, (San Francisco, Harper and Row Publishers, 1983). Wicca correspondences and the Wheel of the Year, I owe to Starhawk, *The Spiral Dance: A Rebirth of the Ancient Religion of the Great Goddess*, (San Francisco, Harper and Row Publishers, 1979). Connections for the Chinese and Goddess calendars are also made to the cosmology of the Hopi Indians, and the reference there is to Frank Waters, *Book of the Hopi*, (New York, Ballantine Books, 1963). A bibliography is included at the end of this book. All of the original Chinese hexagrams and many of the traditional hexagram titles have been revised and changed to implement a philosophy and government system that is very different from the original texts. The version of the *I Ching* or *Book of Changes* that was used in reference to create *The Kwan Yin Book of Changes* was that of Richard Wilhelm and Cary F. Baynes, Translators, in Bollingen Series XIX, (Princeton, Princeton University Press, 1950 and 1967). All direct quotations are referenced in the text.

I would like to thank Brenda Jackson for her editorship and insights in the revising of the first draft of this book. Appreciation and thanks are given too, to Priss Sloss and Kathy Lenhart for their Tarot scholarship that made Appendix II possible, to Vicki Noble for her foreword and caring, to Merlin Stone, and to all of the wonderful people who endorsed and supported this book in press. I offer thanks also to the women of matriarchy and who will read and use *The Kwan Yin Book of Changes* and reclaim her from the male past.

THE KWAN YIN BOOK OF CHANGES:
HOW TO USE HER

Women of matriarchy call upon the *I Ching* for prophecy. She answers questions, analyzes situations, clarifies options. Particularly strong in questions of relationships, she is sister to the Tarot and the Nordic Runes, believed to be at least 3000 years old, and of Chinese origin. In casting *The Kwan Yin I Ching*, the woman who questions is aware of the nature of change as her driving principle. The oracle operates in the present, in what the situation and aspects are at the time of asking. She may reflect the past or future, but only as implicit in the present. She does not predict the definite future, since by the time the future occurs the aspects will have changed. She advises and directs the paths to follow, the possibilities, the choices to make in regard to the situation as she now appears. The woman who seeks may ask the oracle again at a later time, and the new answer reflects changes that have since occurred.

As in any spiritual tool, *The Kwan Yin I Ching* is approached with respect. In asking a question that the seeker has no real wish to know, a foolish question, or in refusing to accept a reading as she is given, the frivolous questioner is admonished. *Youthful Folly*, Hexagram 4, states: "At third request she is not answered". The Superior Woman does not repeat her query again and again in the same reading.

Use of *The Kwan Yin Book of Changes* requires the casting of three two sided objects. Pennies are fine, with their heads side and tails side, but any small two sided object easily thrown from the hand are possible. Two sided objects are necessary, as what is being asked for is a combination of dualities: bright and dark, yin and yang, yes and no. When these objects are thrown six times, the resulting combinations create six lines, and the six lines in their order create a hexagram. Each of the possible sixty-four hexagrams, made by throwing three coins together six times, is a numbered passage in the book.

For example, a woman throws her three pennies and gets two heads and a tail. This is her *bottom* line in the hexagram, and looks like this: ___ ___ (a broken line). This represents yin, the number six, or the negative aspect. She throws the coins a total of six times, and the six lines she draws (going from bottom to top) are her six places in the hexagram figure. The possibilities in her six throws are:

___x___	6	(moving line)	3 tails
_____	7	(young yang)	2 tails, 1 head (changes to 9)
__ __	8	(young yin)	2 heads, 1 tail (changes to 6)
___o___	9	(moving line)	3 heads

If one or more of her casts are three heads or three tails, the result is a moving line. In this case, both of the changes or dualities apply, and the line is both a yin and yang line. This adds an additional hexagram to the reading, adding depth and complexity to the analysis. For example, in the following cast of six lines:

Upper Trigram:
(Above)
(top three lines)

    __ __   Top line (2 heads, 1 tail). Last throw.

    __ __   Fifth line (2 heads, 1 tail)

    ___o___   Fourth line (3 heads, moving line, used as

          _____ or __ __)

Lower Trigram:
(Below)
(bottom three lines)

    __ __   Third line (2 heads, 1 tail)

    _____   Second line (2 tails, 1 head)

    __ __   Bottom line (2 heads, 1 tail) First throw.

The resulting hexagrams are:

Hexagram 7
Shih —
The Women

or

Hexagram 40
Hsieh —
Release

When there is more than one moving line in a reading, the easiest way to handle it is to change all the lines at once. If the six casts look like this:

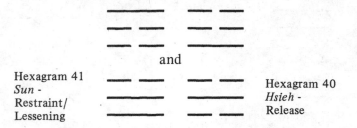

   3 heads (moving line)
   2 heads, one tail (young yin)
   3 tails (moving line)

   2 heads, one tail (young yin)
   2 tails, 1 head (young yang)
   3 heads (moving line)

The two resulting hexagrams are:

and

Hexagram 41
Sun -
Restraint/
Lessening

Hexagram 40
Hsieh -
Release

Three heads is a moving line ——o—— with a value of 9, a yang line. Three tails in a cast is a moving line ——x—— with a value of 6, a yin line, initially. Each changes to her opposite duality, becoming 6 and 9 both. Moving lines are read as ___ ___ and as _____.

By looking at the chart of hexagrams on the inside back cover, the questioner knows which passages to read in the text. In the case of a moving line or lines, she has more than one answer to go by. Two (or more) answers are rarely unrelated or irrelevant to her question. If there are no moving lines within the six casts, the readings are simpler, but the process is the same.

There are eight basic hexagram patterns, and a trigram is a combination of the first three or the second three lines cast. The throwing of three coins has four possible combinations to make a line, and the three lines in a trigram have eight possible combinations. The two trigrams together, six lines or two trigrams, can occur in sixty-four possibilities. Each of the eight basic trigrams is named, and each represents attributes or elements of the *I Ching* and the Goddess.

Each line has a number value of six or nine, and this number value is assigned at the heading of each line within the hexagram text.

THE EIGHT BASIC TRIGRAMS

Ch'ien — The Labyris, Air

K'un — The Pentacle, Earth

K'an — The Chalice, Water

Li — The Wand, Fire

Chen — The Awakening, Thunder

Ken — Keeping Still, Mountain

Sun — The Gentle Wind/Wood

Tui — The Joyous Daughter, Lake

To list the casts as either nine or six, (positive or negative, yin or yang, plus or minus) is to simplify the traditional way of numbering. In the Chinese *I Ching*, the numbers are reduced to sixes and nines ultimately, but do not begin as such. Also, the use of three coins for divination is a modern and western simplification of using yarrow stalks to define and number the lines that comprise a hexagram. Despite the complexities, throwing *The Kwan Yin I Ching* becomes very simple with a little practice. There are fewer aspects than in the Tarot, and the method of reaching the aspects is more set, but the readings are thorough and in depth.

The woman asking for an *I Ching* reading may ask for a "yes" or "no" answer to her question, or for an analysis of a situation. "Is this choice right or wrong? What are my options? What consequences? What direction may I take in this relationship?" *The Kwan Yin Book of Changes* is based on the principle that women control their lives by their own choices and actions. A reading of the oracle is a clarification of choices and possibilities, but she does not determine fate. A hexagram cast that draws a numbered passage of one to thirty will find relations to spirituality and the unconscious. A cast that draws a passage numbered thirty-one to sixty-four will find more emphasis on relationships and daily life, though the aspects often overlap in category. By coming to her in a grounded, centered manner, and by seeking answers with the respect due to any psychic tool, *The Kwan Yin I Ching* will provide much information and many rewards.

A way of approaching this grounded and centered space is through ritual or meditation. Set aside a time and place without distractions, and create an altar of that space. The altar may be simple, containing this *I Ching*, the three coins, and paper and pencil to draw the hexagram. It may also be complex, with white and purple candles, objects to represent each of the seasons or to image the current season and directions. Such objects could include a seashell or chalice for water, autumn and the west; incense, a feather, or athame for air, spring and the east; candles, a wand or an energy crystal for fire, summer and the south; and a stalk of wheat, a rock or an animal figure for the winter pentacle north. Sit straight and comfortably on the floor before the book and altar, light the candles and incense moving clockwise, and take deep and even breaths. Clear all concerns from mind, changing daily reality to stillness and peace.

When calm and centered, the seeker invokes the Goddess. This may de done formally by casting a circle, or simply by repeating her

name or names in the way of the Chinese. Kwan Yin is the women's
Goddess of mercy and of this *I Ching*, and Goddess of peace and
understanding. Ask her to be there, to speak and offer comfort
through this reading: hold her pictured image, feel her presence.

Taking thee pennies or two-sided objects in the left hand, the
seeker cups them in her palm while forming her question silently or
aloud. Allow time for the question to become clear, and ask only one
question in each reading. Repeat and meditate on the query, asking
for knowledge. Transfer the coins to the right hand and cast the
bottom line of the hexagram. Mark the result on paper. Retrieve the
coins, and cast them five more times.

Locate the hexagram in the table on the inside back cover, and
open *The Kwan Yin Book of Changes* to the reading. Read the hexagram slowly, relating the question to the season, passage and overall
summary given in the Introduction, The Center and Reflection. Read
the Movement, where a series of choices, aspects, or progression of
actions is given. Meditate on the reading for as long as necessary, and
reread the hexagram. When the meaning is clear and the seeker satisfied, thank the Goddess or Goddesses invoked, open the circle, blow
out the candles, or go on to another reading.

In the traditional Chinese, women approach knowledge through
Kwan Yin directly, while men make their queries through her Priestess. Men wishing to approach the oracle without help do so through
invoking first the feminine principle in themselves. They may use or
vary the above ritual, calling on the Goddess as she dwells within them,
and using the *I Ching* to strengthen that aspect of their lives.

In the same vein, *The Kwan Yin Book of Changes* is a Wheel of
the Year meditation cycle. Appendix I connects the Chinese months
to the Western Zodiac and Wiccan Sabbat calendars, as well as to the
Hopi Road of Life. Select the hexagram number corresponding to
the sabbat or ritual, do an invoking ritual as above, with emphasis on
the Wheel and on the time, and use seasonal objects for the altar. No
coins are cast. Read and meditate on the material in each hexagram.

Understanding the interconnectedness of all life is a goal in using
the *I Ching* as a meditation cycle. The seasons are marked by sabbats,
signs and ceremonials. These in turn are mirrored in the changing
year, the actual changing earth, and in the ages and changes of all
that lives. The Goddess is the earth and of the earth and "thou art
Goddess". The Wheel turns in contemplation with Kwan Yin's gentle
blessing.

The Hexagrams
Part I

1. CH'IEN / THE CREATIVE UNIVERSE

―――――

Above: Ch'ien — The Labyris, Air

―――――

Below: Ch'ien — The Labyris, Air

Ch'ien's six positive lines are the beginning idea of women's spirituality, the Goddess as maiden thought-form, the labyris of the creative. She is the idea and the action that manifests; she is the wind-carrier, immanence, the generative force. The image is of the universe, energy as flow and creation both in and unrestrained by time. Time and the power of timelessness is the strength of continuing, the circle of being that is the Goddess.

Goddess in woman's universe is both movement and potential of the earth herself and of women in matriarchy. In cosmic terms, the hexagram states the power and harmony of creativity. In matriarchal terms, she states the spiraling of divine action on women's lives, as through the labyris of the High Priestess spirituality is channeled on earth. The Goddess is the earth and *of* the earth; the matriarchy and her spirituality are woman and all women. In the raising up of power, these are one.

The sword, athame or labyris represents the powers of creative air. By the thought-form all begins. All aspects of psychic work, of abstraction, thought and learning, are ruled by air and symbolized by the labryis, and Swords are a suit in the Tarot. The sun rises in the east; her colors of clear light and early hope are the beginnings of the creative universe, of spirituality, of the labyris principles of air.

15

THE CENTER – Women's Spirituality. Blessings.

> The Goddess is
> Transcendent power.
> Continuing peace.

In casting this oracle, the answer is peace that arrives through universal harmony. Strength is gained by seeking the benefit of all women along with oneself, by continuing in what is good and correct. Potential, transcendence and enduring power are qualities of the Goddess and of the hexagram *Ch'ien*; they are attainable in women's lives.

All that exists begins as idea. The tree lies in the seed and the life force grows; the labyris waits to be forged from ore. By connection with the cycles of creation, the woman or matriarchy gains spirituality and truth. Strength lies in understanding that all things are connected, that the laws of the creative universe are the laws of women's lives. Each step taken creatively furthers the Goddess' natural order. Time becomes timeless and seed becomes oak; the metal is discovered and transformed.

The Spiritual Woman brings strength and peace to the matriarchy by actions that shape and recognize order. From ores of power hidden in earth, she creates the labyris of women's empowerment and change. Her ideas utilize materials, turn them from thought to reality. The High Priestess holds the labyris high in the circle as a symbol: by the powers of imagination, all things become possible and real. The ore is idea and the labyris is form; the ore is women and the labyris is matriarchy. The universal and creative mirror the individual, the galaxy mirrors the earthly, and the matriarchy mirrors the women within her. "As above us, so below."*

REFLECTION

> The labyris of
> Creative power:
> The Spiritual Woman
> Transcends, endures.

The trigram for creation is repeated twice in this hexagram and

---

*Principle wiccan saying.

indicates the motion of the universe. Day ends and another day begins, each year precedes another year. The result of movement is time; the continuing of movement is timelessness. Unending endurance is in time and transcends her, an action of movement that continues beyond reckoning. This principle is the creative, the power of air.

In the way of the creative, the Spiritual Woman develops her ideas into skills. She grows in power and harmony by training the good in herself, by raising up a labyris of shining strength. She gains an unswerving endurance that brings her goals into reach. In matriarchy, the community grows by flowing with cosmic law.

MOVEMENT

*Nine at the beginning:**
>Unutilized potential.
>The dragon's powers
>Wait.

The dragon is a creature of air and the Chinese symbol of power and awakening. She is active energy, light and lightning, life. She is the labyris potentialized by the unmined ore, and one of many aspects of the Goddess. In winter the dragon waits below ground. Like the Goddess in springtime, she returns and the life force ascends.

Hidden in the sleeping center, the dragon is quiet but aware; the labyris waits. Appearing in women's terms, she is a skilled Mother who is not yet recognized in her forms, her skills are unutilized but ready. Secure in her power and potential, she bides her time with stillness. Power spent too soon is force, and force is to be avoided. Actions come correctly in their time.

Nine in the second place:
>The dragon is seen.
>The Spiritual Woman
>Begins.

Power begins to appear and spark. The breeze dawns with spring, the dragon stirs. The Spiritual Woman begins her circle as a woman of matriarchy. Her strength is discovered by her Sisters, and her knowledge, empowerment, openness and integrity are recognized. She changes her place for the better, both on earth and in the community. Now is the time to begin.

---

*The beginning is always the bottom line, the first line that is cast.

Nine in the third line:
>She works all day.
>At night she does not rest.
>Caution but no error.

The Spiritual Woman is accepted by her matriarchy and her skills are put to use; the ore is mined and forged. She has responsibilities and cares, and when others sleep, she works and worries. She takes caution and is not overwhelmed. There is danger in influence, but true spirituality remains unaffected. She who stays connected with creative harmony avoids error.

Nine in the fourth position:
>A choice impends.
>Two pathways,
>Both correct.

At a point of motion between changes, choice begins. The Spiritual Woman either rises to leadership as a Mother in matriarchy, or chooses inward development as a Priestess. Both are valid choices on the Wheel of Life. The Spiritual Woman decides by the laws of her own spiral. She acts from centered harmony, and finds the way to happiness that benefits herself and all. Her choice is correct in either direction and she chooses well.

Nine in the fifth place:
>The dragon flies
>And lands on earth.
>All benefit.

The Spiritual Woman learns transcendence, and is followed by the matriarchy. The flow of the Goddess' universe is channeled through her to the earth. She learns and she teaches. She is strong in thought and action, and in love. All who approach her are benefited and she turns no Sister away. The Goddess is pleased with her Daughter's choices and grants her success.

Nine at the top:
>Ambition sets
>Her apart.
>She errs.

This line is a reminder of humility. When a woman gains, she does not fly so high that she forgets her earth beginnings. She does not lose touch or connectedness with the Wheel of Life, or she finds herself alone. Isolation leads to failure and is prevented. The Spiritual Woman is aware, grounded and humble in transcendence: good fortune begins and continues.

A NOTE ON NINES

> Six lines are nines:
> A tapestry of
> Flying dragons.
> They change.

A tapestry of dragons is airborne and in motion, six dragons embroidered on a Chinese robe by women's hands, six dragons for the six positive lines of the hexagram. Total motion becomes total receptivity and *Ch'ien* becomes *K'un*, Hexagram 2. The strength of the universe, of the labyris, air, the dragon of hidden potential, becomes the giving devotion of the manifest earth. The gentleness of the earth, the pentacle, mirrors the creative life force of the universe, the labyris, and both are one. The Maiden/High Priestess aspect of *Ch'ien, the Creative Universe* becomes the Mother Goddess/Empress of *K'un, The Receptive Earth*. Good fortune and empowerment results from this turning of the Wheel. Perfect love and perfect trust are women's spirituality and spiritual strength.

2. K'UN / THE RECEPTIVE EARTH

—— ——
—— ——   *Above*: K'un — The Pentacle, Earth
—— ——

—— ——
—— ——   *Below*: K'un — The Pentacle, Earth
—— ——

K'un's six unshortened lines represent the element earth. Earth is dark and physical, she is fertile in becomings of female gentleness, of nourishment and devotion. All things in *K'un* are counterpart dualities to Hexagram 1, *Ch'ien*. The two hexagrams are the contradictions in all life and in the universe. *K'un* is peace and waiting, fullness and completion, receptivity, pregnancy and the night. She is all of the qualities that are continuations and opposites of *The Creative Universe*, the primal ideas of mind and air made real on earth.

This hexagram is The Empress in the Tarot, the Mother aspect of the Goddess, the full moon. Taurus, Virgo and Capricorn are her astrological signs. Her names in part are Ceres, Selene, Isis, Demeter, Aphrodite, Ishtar, Mawu Lisa, Gaia and Rhiannon. She is the force of mature growth, nature and the physical body, birth, death, mountains, and the material world.*

The pentacle is the five pointed star of wicca, and symbolizes the connectedness of the four earth directions with air or spirit. The aspects of air and earth, labyris and pentacle, Maiden and Mother, are dualities that are one. When *Ch'ien* expresses early beginnings and thought-forms, *K'un* is the thought-form materialized. She is the mature and bearing female aspect, the concrete world. In matriarchal terms, earth portrays the role of the Mother, the grounded and wise leader of the women's community. She is the pentacle of love, power, wisdom, justice, knowledge,† the four directions and the air, that are the qualities of women's spirituality made real. Pentacles as a suit in the Tarot represent all aspects of the physical plane, the sustenance of the life force. As symbols of creation, birth and rebirth, the economic and physical world, and the fullness of the harvest, pentacles also affirm and validate women's community. They represent bonds between women, between Mother and Daughter and among Sisters,†† and represent matriarchy as a whole.

THE CENTER – The Pentacle Full Moon. Fulfillment.

> Fulfillment through
> Receptive strength.
> She who follows leads.

The Receptive has earthly reality, the image of the mare. The mare is grounded, strong, swift and free-roaming; she is gentle and open and loving. Her complement, the dragon in *Ch'ien*, partakes of her opposites. But the mare was created along with the dragon, and

---

*Starhawk, *The Spiral Dance: A Rebirth of the Ancient Religion of the Great Goddess*, (San Francisco, Harper and Row Publishers, 1979), p. 203.
†*Ibid.*, p. 66.
††Vicki Noble, *Motherpeace: A Way to the Goddess Through Myth, Art and Tarot*, (San Francisco, Harper and Row Publishers, 1983), p. 156.

creativity is key to both. The life force generates and sustains all things in beauty, creates from the active labyris of air, and brings to birth from the pentacle of the earth.

On earth, in women's lives, *K'un* signifies action or waiting as dependent upon situation. There is a time for each, and each is fulfilled in her time. The Superior Woman knows when to seek guidance; she knows when she does not know. If she approaches her karma with receptivity, she knows how to meet and to influence her fate. When there is much to be accomplished, the Superior Woman does not overextend her resources, but turns to her Mothers and Sisters for aid. The receptive and creative, the earth and the universe, the pentacle and the brought-to-creation labyris are one. In knowing her position on the spiral of the Goddess, the Superior Woman achieves fulfillment.

REFLECTION

> Earth carries all:
> Receptivity in her time.
> The Superior Woman
> Carries the world.

The trigram representing the pentacle is repeated twice, symbolizing undiluted power. Earth, the pentacle, supports and nourishes all that lives and brings all life to birth and death. She reconciles the contradictions without question, and represents all aspects of natural order and law. As earth supports all, so the Superior Woman on her planet learns openness and acceptance. She learns strength, integrity, sustenance, patience and enduring. In her inner devotion, the Superior Woman, likening to the strength and receptivity of the earth, supports and nourishes the matriarchy with her skills and virtues. The receptive aspect of woman is intrinsic in the pentacle from which she came; she takes the creativity of her thought-forms and makes them real on earth.

MOVEMENT

> *Six at the beginning:*
> At the equinox
> Winter nears.

The earth and pentacle, represented through sunset and fall, image the death-nearing aspect and the body. One follows the other in a cycle of cycles that become the universe. With the equinox in September, winter's power begins to manifest. After a time of red glowing leaves, a time of fulfillment and harvest, comes the hard cold of death and dormancy. New beginnings follow these ends, but cannot happen without them.

In women's lives the cycles follow the years. The Mother follows the Maiden and the Crone follows the Mother. Final decay and final death approach. But living is reborn in springtime and the Wheel turns once more.

Six in the second line:
A pentacle within the circle.
All prosper.

As the circle represents the universe, so does the pentacle represent the earth within her. A hexagram and circle are both formed from the point and the line, and lines indicate movement. The pentacle and circle are thus one, the universe and the earth, the macrocosm and the microcosm.

What is natural is good: this is represented by the circle. Calm and stillness represent the star. Receptivity and the equality of all creation within the natural cycle is spirituality and transcendence. The earth achieves what is good without craft or exception: what exists is what there is. The matriarchy and every woman within her achieve connectedness through natural order. Matriarchy is the circle within the circle, and the Superior Woman is the star within the star. By mirroring the receptive strength of the pentacle, matriarchy achieves success.

Six in the third position:
Restraint.
Her work becomes foundation.

The Superior Woman gives what she can within her skills but does not try to channel powers she is unable to control. With restraint and modesty she grows to wisdom. She does not seek recognition prematurely or undeservedly. In her workings, she lays foundations for the future by what she does today.

Six in the fourth place:
> A black hole in space.
> Do not act.

A black hole opens at her actions, and hesitation is not wrong. In a dangerous situation, the Superior Woman does not seek to be noticed or to activate negative forces. She remains watchful and calm and her peril withdraws. She hides within the crowd by stillness.

Six in the fifth line:
> The color yellow.
> Fulfillment.

Yellow represents earth, the pentacle, a symbol of the mid-stage of the galaxy. The universe is above and the center is below, the world is in between. In matriarchy, when a woman is called upon by the Mothers to take action, success and fulfillment depend on her behavior as much as on her skills. From a middle place of responsibility, the Superior Woman proves herself reliable for higher level work. Her integrity and development, maturity and groundedness, are apparent in decisions and results. She does not have to point out her worth.

Six at the top:
> Darkness meets light.
> Neither wins.

Dark and light, fall and spring, earth and universe: the receptive and creative are complementary opposites. There is a place for each and each has her place in the Goddess' order. One cannot replace the other, and both manifest at once. Women's law follows the universe, and the matriarchy is fulfilled.

A NOTE ON SIXES

Six lines are sixes:
> Continuity, harmony,
> Success.

Six mares run swiftly over the earth, sparks striking from their hooves as they hit the ground. There are six receptive lines to this hexagram. When the lines are all sixes, they change to all nines, and *K'un, the Receptive Earth* becomes *Ch'ien, The Creative Universe*. The creative mind, the labyris, becomes the manifesting principle of the earth, the pentacle. By this means, the active and receptive are a single positive force in the universe and matriarchy.

3. CHUN / BEGINNINGS

Above: K'an — The Chalice, Water

Below: Chên — The Awakening, Thunder

Chun is the child pushing her way toward light. She is the pain
and beauty of beginnings, the meeting of earth with the stars. *Chen*,
the lower trigram, is awakening; her upward motion is signified by
thunder. *K'an* in the upper trigram, is water, the source and depths
of all life, represented by earthward movement and signified by rain.
Together, the trigrams image the moment of birth, the excitement of
a thunderstorm, the energy of new life. The Daughter, head crowned
with the final throes of labor, enters the world and begins her first
cries. Her head lifts to breathe the light; labor ceases beyond crisis
and living begins.

THE CENTER — A New Day. Beginnings.

> The moment of birth.
> Beginnings.
> Patience and progress.
> She is not alone.

Awakenings are chaotic times; births and rebirths do not occur
in stillness. She is struggling to gain new forms and this is motion and
action. From her struggles come success and blessings. When a woman
begins or awakens to a new level of knowledge, she initiates her transformations from the dark. Out of darkness comes the dawn, out of
winter comes the springtime. The woman in her newness, however,

recognizes that she is new; in her new state she is young and innocent, she makes no impulsive moves. Until she understands and learns her new skills, she is not left unguided. She does not look to her Mothers to make decisions for her, but looks to them for advice before she acts. With wisdom and nurturing, the woman begings a new dawn.

REFLECTION

> A massing storm:
> The labor of beginnings.
> The Superior Woman
> Finds balance in chaos.

The coming thunderstorm represents the energy of new awakening, but order is there and is acknowledged. Contradictions are one, they both exist. The Superior Woman recognizes that turmoil and new births are an order in themselves. She places and sorts the abundance around her, as Psyche once sorted the sand from the grain. To find balance in her world, the Superior Woman learns to divide and to bring together. She learns that the two are one.

MOVEMENT

> *Nine at the beginning:*
> Awareness of obstacles.
> She is determined
> And asks help.

Birth is a primal force but not accomplished easily. She occurs with labor and obstacles, but occurs inevitably and always strongly. The woman awakening is certainly born, but does not force nature against her time or the manner of her process. She continues to grow steadily, without forcing herself ahead or holding back. She seeks her guides with dignity and temperance. By knowledge of her newness, she gains what she needs to learn.

> *Six in the second line:*
> Obstacles increase.
> A turning about.
> Success in time.

The Superior Woman finds every encounter new to her, and sees obstacles on all sides. Her affairs reverse themselves again and again, but what seems to be hindrances may not be. When the time is right, she finds her guides. When the guide is right for the woman, both know.

> *Six in the third place:*
>   The Superior Woman
>   Knows when to act
>   And when to hold back.

A woman is new to the community and cannot find her path. She does not walk in circles but asks for help, and with the aid of her Sisters finds what she needs. If she acts alone too soon, she fails, but with guides to advise her and knowing when the time is right, the Superior Woman begins.

> *Six in the fourth position:*
>   She begins at
>   Her beginnings.
>   Furthering flow.

The woman recognizes a time of action, but thinks she does not know how. Risk is taken without timidity or arrogance. By bringing herself to begin, to take the first initiative, her situation opens and she sees what to do next. To seek advice is neither wrong nor weak, but the Superior Woman makes her own decisions.

> *Nine in the fifth place:*
>   Cautious action.
>   Gentle continuance.
>   Eventual success.

Obstacles bend her meanings and actions; she moves slowly and with great care. This is not the time for force, but for the gaining of support that makes achievement possible. By steady and gentle continuance, she raises the obstacles that block her. Her situation slowly clarifies; she begins to reach her goals.

> *Six at the top:*
>   Overwhelming beginnings.
>   Temporary setbacks.
>   She does not act.

Some beginnings are more difficult than others. A woman

becomes afraid, feels blocked, cannot find the right guides or Mothers to help her. She quits; she goes back into the earth of becomings to hide. When the time comes, new growth proceeds and the Daughter emerges into light. Births and awakenings are necessary and inevitable — in their time. If she cannot act now, she waits for when she can. The failure is not a failure, and does not prevail. The Superior Woman knows when a setback leads to success; she waits for her moment and prevails.

4. MÊNG / YOUTHFUL FOLLY

— — —
— — —
— — —

Above: Kên — Keeping Still, Mountain

— — — — —
— — —
— — —

Below: K'an — The Chalice, Water

This hexagram is of innocence rather than blame, as symbolized by The Fool in the Tarot. The trigrams show the stillness of waiting mountains and the flowing of water. Water flowing from the root of a mountain is the Chinese symbol of youthful innocence. In the Motherpeace Tarot deck, the Fool is shown blissfully walking on her hands into a mountain stream, unaware of the depths and perils that surround her. Water, the lower trigram, flows and as she does so she fulfills and grows strong. Triumph and joy in innocence are achieved.

THE CENTER — Childhood Walks Where Mothers Fear. Success.

> The child asks a question:
> At first request the Mothers answer.
> At second request the Mothers answer.
> At third request she is not answered.

In childhood, foolishness is not wrong. The Daughter learns by her errors. She finds a Mother to teach her and her attitude is good. She learns modesty, interest and respect for age. The Mother who teaches the Daughter waits for the child to approach. The child asks for help in her time.

The teacher's response to questions is simple and honest, and the child accepts what is given. The Daughter's persistence in repeating her question provokes her teacher, until the Mother refuses to answer.

A child asks until her curiosity and understanding are satisfied. Thus she learns what she needs to know at last. Real learning is success. This hexagram refers to the Mother who teaches, as well as to the Daughter who seeks learning and is taught.

REFLECTION

> The Daughter nurses
> From the spring of life:
> The Superior Woman grows
> With all she learns.

The image of the hexagram is of a spring flowing at the base of a mountain, or a child nursing at the breast. As the infant draws life from the universe of her Mother's body, so she draws learning from the wellspring of her Mother's wisdom. By this flowing outward, this sharing of knowledge and experience from Mother to Daughter, innocence becomes responsible in the matriarchy. The foolish child becomes a Sister and then a Mother herself, and the circle of life continues on.

MOVEMENT

> *Six at the beginning:*
> To teach the child
> The Mothers set limits.
> The limits remain wise.

Boundaries begin education, and moderation is learning. The Daughter takes everything as play, and understands no gravity. Restraint is called for, but the Mothers are not harsh. She who knows only playing does not succeed at living, but she who knows only seriousness has lost too much. In each of the Mothers there is still a little child.

Nine in the second place:
    Patience with Daughters,
    And gentleness with children.
    The Mothers teach success.
The Mother who teaches a Daughter has the patience and strength
to be gentle. She knows the weakness of every woman's folly. She
recognizes the innocent's true spirit and praises her Daughter fully.
With inner clarity and outward reserve, the Mothers likewise lead
the matriarchy.

Six in the third position:
    Protect the child
    Who cannot protect herself.
    Continuing flow.
A newly awakening Daughter is easily submerged by a stronger
woman's nature. Such childish innocence harbors a crush or acts
recklessly, to the detriment of herself and her teacher. A Daughter
gains self-respect by waiting until approached. She courts rebuff who
offers herself unwanted, and the Mother is inappropriate who accepts
her unwisdom.

Six in the fourth line:
    Woven fantasies.
    The child suffers
    Humiliation.
In youth there is pain in living by realities that truth uncovers in
time. The child suffers, torn between what she believes and what is
real. The harder she holds on, the stronger her hurt as she lets go of
her fantasies. The Mother knows when to leave her Daughter alone,
when to spare or not to spare her this time of pain. In her indignity
the child acquires wisdom and becomes a woman. The Mothers know
when to wait.

Six in the fifth place:
    Youthful folly
    And innocence
    Affirmed.
The Daughter who asks for teaching learns success. Her attitude

is of meekness and open receptivity. She who approaches the Mothers without prideful assuming, learns and grows in joy.

> *Nine at the top:*
>> In restraining the Daughter,
>> The Mother knows
>> When to stop.

The impetuous Daughter is sometimes forced into seriousness. This restraint is unlike the beginning setting of boundaries. Limits, however necessary are not imposed without reason or established in anger, and are confined to the uses of temperance. Punishment is never physical and is never self-justified. In the matriarchy, intervention is solely to preserve balance. The Daughter is made free to learn.

5. HSÜ / WAITING NOURISHMENT

Above: K'an — The Chalice, Water

Below: Ch'ien — The Labyris, Air

Ch'ien, the labyris of air, supports the trigram for water and the chalice, *K'an*. Women seek the waters of spirituality, and the chalice fills when she is ready. As ocean waves lap the shore, or rain-nourished streams flow to fill a lake, inner nourishment enters women's lives. The Spiritual Woman knows when to wait, and is ready to receive when nourishment comes to her. In times of uncertainty, though water surrounds her, the chalice remains unfilled.

THE CENTER — Nourishment in Time. She Flows.

> With enduring
> Comes nourishment.
> Proceed and flow.

Waiting is the sureness of nourishment, the certainty of hope. A positive outlook leads the Spiritual Woman to good outcome, and affirms the power of her certainty.

An unknown is faced, a depth that contains danger and stress. Fear and anger do not help her. The empowered woman accepts her required cares and flows to successful ends. Her nourishment comes from within, her cup of life. She is realistic with herself and her situation, but when obstacles are met clearly and directly, the best channels become known. The Spiritual Woman, nourished by the fluid depths of inner truth, takes strong and certain action. She faces danger and prevails.

REFLECTION

> Water and air:
> She fills her chalice.
> The Spiritual Woman
> Is nourished.

Water flows, and nothing hurries or prevents her from reaching the sea. In women's lives, actions and decisions proceed in time to turn her life where she wants to go. When the time is right, she acts to fill her chalice, but not before. Worry does not help her, nor does anxiety or fear. The Spiritual Woman nourishes herself with the life-cup of inner clarity; she flows. She remains positive and she waits. When the time for action comes, she is ready to swim and to fulfill.

MOVEMENT

> *Nine at the beginning:*
> She waits on land
> And continues.
> No error.

The danger is still at low tide and the woman works on her land. Things are changing, they begin to flow. The Spiritual Woman continues with her daily life while she may. In doing so, she conserves herself for what comes.

> *Nine in the second place:*
> She waits on the dunes
> Of discord.
> Eventual flow.

The tide approaches. Currents shift beneath her feet and the waters are rapid and unknown. There is discord and conflict among women. The Spiritual Woman remains calm and holds her cup. She does not add to disharmony and she succeeds.

Nine in the third line:
    She waits on the shore
    And is stuck.
    The issue arrives.

The shore is undermined by unbound waves, and the woman is stuck on the beach. She has acted at the wrong time and not contained her strength. She cannot cross the channel or fill her chalice with clear water. Dangers break on her vulnerability and she reacts. The Spiritual Woman is cautious now; her consciousness saves the day.

Six in the fourth position:
    She sees riptides,
    And escapes
    However she can.

The woman is out of her depth and the crisis is now. There is no way out but through. She struggles to stand in the tide and sees herself washed away. She endures, remains calm and she swims. She waits and holds her own. This is not the time to fill or nourish.

Nine in the fifth place:
    She waits the cup of
    Inner nourishment.
    Calm waters.

In a moment of calm waters, the Spiritual Woman floats and marshals her strength and resources. By accepting flow without losing sight of the shoreline, the Spiritual Woman fulfills to success. She is sure of her triumph, and swims in her time.

Six at the top:
    She swims to shore
    And is rescued.
    Good outcome.

The time is now and is fulfilled; the woman swims toward shore. When she is safe, her Sisters arrive. She suspects their motives but receives them with respect. By her correct manner they aid her and she fills her cup. Danger is turned to good outcome by acceptance of the means. The Spiritual Woman is nourished and supported in the flow of life. Help comes unlooked for; she is safe on land.

6. HUNG / CONFLICT

Above: Ch'ien – The Labyris, Air

Below: K'an – The Chalice, Water

Ch'ien represents the expanding universe, the labyris air moving outward. *K'an*, the lower trigram, is water, the chalice of life, moving on inner planes. The ideas present a conflict of motion, but in nature they do not contradict or impede. Resolution and conflict are two aspects, and one is implicit in the other. In women's nature, the depths and flow of water combine with the creativity of universal order. The woman with these qualities is the strength and wisdom of matriarchy; she is a Mother in communal government and a Priestess in the spiritual core.

THE CENTER – Harmony in Conflict. Change.

> The woman is honest
> But faces conflict.
> She waits for change.

The woman's path holds obstacles, but she knows her course is good. She presents her ideas to her Sisters for resolution by consensus, and her ideas to the Mothers for discussion and learning. During conflict, she remains centered and clear. If she knows her path is still correct, she compromises and waits. In unity there is blessing; in conflict the matriarchy suffers. Consensus and guidance turn conflict into resolution, and resolution brings new growth.

REFLECTION

> The outward and inward universe:
> Conflict is the image.
> The Superior Woman
> Seeks balance.

The source of conflict is in the apparent opposition of the trigrams' movements, but the depths and heights need not conflict. If the spirituality of women in matriarchy blends, and freedoms and obligations are shared by all, the Sisters stay close to the Wheel of Life. If the women remain connected, there can be no serious imbalance or conflict. In the beginnings of life, as in the cycles of earth and universe, conflict becomes unity and is resolved.

MOVEMENT

> *Six at the beginning:*
> She does not stir.
> Little debate.
> Eventual success.

In the beginnings of conflict, the Superior Woman waits for developments. A decision is not rushed without full information. There is good fortune if she does not speak.

> *Nine in the second place:*
> She does not participate.
> She compromises and waits.
> No censure.

Withdrawal from conflict is wisdom. If she errs, she bows to her Sisters' greater understanding. If she is correct, they see her views in time. She does not prevail alone. The Superior Woman avoids discord when she may.

> *Six in the third line:*
> What a woman possesses
> By integrity
> Cannot be taken away.

Spiritual skills once gained cannot be taken away or lost, nor can the innate learnings of a woman's personality or education. These things are there for her to use for her own and the matriarchy's benefit, and for her Sisters to learn and be helped by. The Superior Woman resolves disunity by giving of her skills. She does not seek status or reward.

> *Nine in the fourth place:*
> The Superior Woman
> Revises her outlook
> And is affirmed.

A woman who has not found inner worth participates in dissension and conflict. She could prevail, but cannot succeed by this attitude. Realizing this, the Superior Woman finds space to work within her matriarchy or her circle of women. She is respected and grows in self-image and her attitude changes. Consensus and accord are achieved and she is affirmed.

> *Nine in the fifth position:*
> A mediator is chosen.
> Through objectivity,
> Resolution.

A woman who is able to be objective, and who has the skill to soothe and judge for the good of the group, is chosen to mediate. She settles disputes to agreement, and brings about peace.

> *Nine at the top:*
> Conflict carried
> To fruition.
> No happiness.

A woman who carries conflict to fruition has no victory. She has forced her way but has lost the good will of her Sisters. The outcome is conflict without resolution, and the vital change has not occurred. The matriarchy suffers and the women suffer with her. Resolution is urgently needed.

7. SHIH / THE WOMEN (SISTERS)

Above: K'un — The Pentacle, Earth

Below: K'an — The Chalice, Water

The trigram for water, *K'an* is located under the trigram for earth, and images an underground lake. Women's resources are pooled in matriarchy as an underground well. They are there as needed, and are the wellspring of matriarchal strength. The qualities of the trigrams flow in receptive harmony, the qualities of a consensus population. The women are Sisters in community and are the life source and endurance of matriarchy.

THE CENTER — Women are Matriarchy. Blessings.

> The women flow
> From the source.
> Matriarchy prospers
> And blesses.

The women are individuals with individual needs who become a nation for the good of all. To do so, each participates in the starting and running of matriarchy; they build and create her by their own empowerment. With the consensus leadership of the Mothers communally and the Priestesses spiritually, the Sisters learn to work together and utilize their skills. They are confident in their goals and in each other. They choose as Mothers women who are skilled in order; they choose as Priestesses women who are connected in the cycles of the universe. The Sisters develop a system of moral justice by these lights, and they work by consensus to decide how the matriarchy is run. Each woman has skills that benefit the community, and no skills are wasted. With goodness, equality and continuing, matriarchy succeeds.

REFLECTION

> Water
> In the earth:
> The women.
> The Superior Women.

Water rests within the earth and becomes the source of nourishment, the root of life. The women are the source of matriarchy, without which she could not exist. By their receptivity, matriarchy is established. By their flowing, she grows and is affirmed. By the waters of life that rise to nourish the earth, the earth bears fruit. In matriarchy, the Sisters do the building and creating with skill and devotion. The women together are the birth and nourishment of their world.

MOVEMENT

> *Six at the beginning:*
>   Direction and peace.
>   Good fortune.

In the establishment of matriarchy, direction is essential. The women are not yet unified but they have a clear goal, a reason for seeking each other out. If they learn order early, good fortune results.

> *Nine in the second place:*
>   The Mothers are recognized.
>   Success.

Women who have skills at government, who can organize women and help to unify them, are recognized by the matriarchy. These Mothers help women to direct their goals and to realize the skills that are needed to achieve them. The Sisters are the strength of matriarchy, and the Mothers are the strength of the Sisters.

> *Six in the third line:*
>   The women lead together.
>   Progress.

Matriarchy is composed of and founded by women who live in her. Each has skills she contributes and skills that are needed. Each Sister has her place, and is valued for herself and for her knowledge. Each is matriarchy and the matriarchy is each woman in her. The

Goddess is in all women, and the matriarchy that recognizes her is blessed in strength.

> *Six in the fourth position:*
>   The women hesitate
>   Without remorse.

Matriarchy begins when her women are not yet skilled in government. Some issues are too difficult to address now, as mishandled they could bring about divisiveness. The Mothers, Priestesses and Sisters recognize which issues are not yet to be touched. In recognizing limits and avoiding breaks there is wisdom, and by avoidance of failure the Sisters generate success. Each issue is met in her time.

> *Six in the fifth line:*
>   The women recognize
>   Cosmic order.
>   Prosperity.

In governing matriarchy, women do not go their own ways. The Mothers help all to participate, and each woman's skills are needed and affirmed. The Mothers unify, and the Sisters pool energies to benefit all. By cooperation and wise organization, matriarchy prospers.

> *Six at the top:*
>   The women strengthen.
>   Matriarchy strengthens.

A woman who finds her place in matriarchy grows and gains in skills. Her Mothers and Sisters watch her strengthen and support her growth. Her skills are made use of and respected. She gains in confidence, self-worth and knowledge, and in her gifts to all. The matriarchy gains from the women within her.

8. PI / HOLDING TOGETHER (UNION)

```
___  ___
_____        Above : K'an — The Chalice, Water
___  ___

___  ___
___  ___        Below :  K'un — The Pentacle, Earth
___  ___
```

In *Holding Together (Union)*, women find completeness in the joining of their lives. The five short lines of this hexagram represent receptivity, the union of women with each other. The single long line, strength line, is in the leading place, suggesting that love is held by women's strength. Raindrops become rivulets, become streams. Small streams merge to rivers; rivers merge to become seas. The waters of the earth are gathered together in an earthen jar, a jar made and held by women's hands. Loving is a law and a gathering of waters of the earth, a pooling together of the life force between women.

THE CENTER — Union Brings Success. Bright Blessings.

> Holding together brings success.
> Union in caring:
> Women who hope come together.
> She who resists is to blame.

Women unite as lovers and in matriarchy that all may affirm and strengthen. Such holding together requires caring and mutual respect. In matriarchy, the Mothers foster cooperation and regard among Sisters to merge the women under common goals. Two individuals meet as lovers. They pool their experiences, their natures and their resources, and they join in each other's love. The waters of streams become one stream, and they merge in the pentacle of earth.

REFLECTION

> The earth is covered by water:
> Holding together in union.
> The women of matriarchy
> Strengthen love's law.

The earth is three-quarters water, and the waters merge on earth. Thus women in a women's society blend, with each member as an individual and as part of the whole. Every Sister's benefit lies in the holding together of matriarchy, and each woman shares in this task. In the union of individuals, women hold together with love.

MOVEMENT

> *Six at the beginning:*
> Holding her honestly,
> The potter's jar.
> Respect and love.

Truth is the way to hold friendship. In the woman-made jar, the waters of life are blended and based in the thought-form of love. Inner strength and honesty attract caring from all around her. Respect and love bring fulfillment.

> *Six in the second place:*
> Holding her
> Spiritually.
> Continuing flow.

If a woman is empowered to act with tact, her position in matriarchy or with her lover is affirmed. If she wastes herself and her loving recklessly, she is incorrect. The Superior Woman never loses her spiritual grace.

> *Six in the third position:*
> She holds together
> And unites
> Falsely.

Women are not drawn into relationships by convenience only, or misfortune results. A Woman who is not her lover becomes her valued friend instead. By adopting false relationships with the wrong woman, she is not aware when her true love appears.

Six in the fourth line:
    Holding her openly
    And with pride.
    Celebration.

Women's bonds with their chosen Mothers are cordial and strong. In matriarchy, women show their caring openly. The community's members are met with joyful pride. The Superior Woman's relations with her lover and her Sisters are spontaneous, warm and good.

Nine in the fifth place:
    The effects of union.
    Those who come
    Come freely.

Consensus rules the workings of matriarchy and the relationships between Sisters. Force does not exist. Freedom validates the structure of society and the lives of her lovers. Clarity and inner wisdom affirm strength and peace. She who comes to matriarchy or to a lover, comes of her own free will.

Six at the top:
    She finds beginnings
    And furthers them.
    Triumphant unity.

The Superior Woman recognizes the beginnings of love. If her timing is off, if she hesitates to act or to give of her devotion, she regrets her waiting later. The woman who recognizes when the time is right is the woman who achieves unity, the holding together of the waters in the earthen jar. She achieves love in her woman's time.

9. HSIAO CH'U / THE CLEANSING WIND

Above: Sun — The Gentle Wind/Wood

Below: Ch'ien — The Labyris, Air

The image is of wind stirring through clouds, rearranging their forms, cleansing the sky, bringing about rain and change. The wind transforms; she is the principle of labyris, air. This hexagram represents the active mind, the unseen forces that control all transformations, the thought-forms of women, the generative power within.

For the Hopi Indian woman, the wind and the element air mean cleansing and healing, the strong cold blast of winter that sweeps away stagnation and emotional depression. Her color is white and her animal is the bear, the healer whose sweep of claw makes everything new. She is the freezing of winter that allows for spring's rebirth. Her direction is north, her jewel the shining lustre of white abalone.

In the western tradition, air rules all aspects of the intellect and mind, the forces of the psychic, intuitive, and the abstract. She is windswept grasslands and beaches, high windy mountain peaks and towers. Her season is spring, her wicca direction east, her jewel topaz, and her time dawn. Air's astrological aspects are Gemini, Libra and Aquarius.*

The Chinese define this hexagram as that of a strong force, the labyris universe, being held back or transformed by a lesser one. The change may be only temporary, and winning depends on the quality of gentleness.

THE CENTER — Change by Slow Measures. Restraint.

The gentle wind
Cleanses and heals.
Good aspects come
By holding back.

---

*Starhawk, _The Spiral Dance: A Rebirth of the Ancient Religion of the Great Goddess_, (San Francisco, Harper and Row Publishers, 1979), p. 201.

This is no time for large actions. Clouds mass, promising cleansing and nourishment, but rain is withheld from the earth. By gentle reasoning and without force, the situation is held within bounds. There are signs of release within blockage and struggle. Through delicate, careful measures the Superior Woman changes her fate. The time is newly begun, and requires slow steadiness and control. Above all, rain lies in holding back.

REFLECTION

> Wind moves the clouds:
> The cleansing wind.
> The Superior Woman
> Creates her temperament.

Wind changes and controls the clouds, directing the rain. Though without form, unsolid and abstract, she has great power for transformations. The Superior Woman, by the winds of her mind and spirituality, creates her outer worlds. To do so, she cultivates her intellect and intuition, and thereby shapes who she is.

MOVEMENT

Nine at the beginning:
> Returnings.
> Good effects.

A strong woman is active by temperament and challenges her fates. However, she finds herself blocked. By returning to reserve, by holding back the impulse to thrust herself forward, she is freer to take careful action. Small steps rather than revolutionary changes have greater effects in the end.

Nine in the second position:
> She follows her Sisters
> And withdraws.

Aggressive action is against peace and involves obstacles. Rather than worry her Sisters, the Superior Woman heeds their warnings. She gains success because she knows when to withdraw.

Nine in the third place:
　Externals hinder.
　She does not act.
Restraints appear small, but the woman takes action by force. Strength lies in mental creativity, and physical energy fails. The mind brings greater victory than muscle. The woman argues with her Sisters, who despair at her lack of awareness. She waits or loses respect.

Six in the fourth line:
　Sincere objectivity.
　Blocks vanish.
The Sister who is confidante to the Superior Woman guides her to correctness. By doing so, she jeopardizes herself. Truth is hardier than any obstruction and triumphs. Through the women's devotion and integrity, good outcome is gained. The Superior Woman chooses a superior Sister, and prevails.

Nine in the fifth position:
　Honest devotion.
　They celebrate.
The Superior Woman accepts restraints from her Sister. In friendship, each partner matches the other, and they bond together in honest devotion. The active woman learns caution and subtlety from her quieter Sister; the thoughtful woman learns how and when to act. In their sharing and loving they are one, and the more that they give, the more that they have for giving. Conflicts reach resolve and the women celebrate.

Nine at the top:
　Rainfall.
　The woman rests.
The wind brings rain from the clouds and peace approaches. A climax is gained by the gathering of small deeds. Release, however, is tenuous and is not taken for granted. Unseen forces have brought change, cleansing, a healing of despair. To continue now could unbalance this. The Superior Woman knows when to rest.

10. LÜ / TREADING SOFTLY (CORRECTNESS)

Above: Ch'ien — The Labyris, Air

Below: Tui — The Joyous Daughter, Lake

The hexagram addresses political correctness in the matriarchy. To bridge the gap between greater and lesser, the labyris of air above and the joyous daughter of the lower trigram, correctness is required. The hexagram also refers to a Daughter treading on the patience of the mighty universe, in the sense that all women are Daughters of the Great Mother's forbearance. That the innocent risk the wrath of power is not perilous in this case. Because she occurs without defiance, in a Daughter's spirit of simplicity and laughter, the universe treats her kindly.

THE CENTER — The Innocent Approach Power. Welcome.

> Treading on the
> Serpent's tail.
> Correctness and
> She does not strike.

The Daughter walks behind a powerful serpent and trips on her tail. The serpent, recognizing the child's smallness, does not strike. She accepts the Daughter gently, as she would her own young. In matriarchy, women are powerful and treat each other with respect, correctness and a sense of humor. Gentleness welcomes and prospers.

REFLECTION

> The labyris over the lake:
> Treading.
> Power tempered with correctness
> Values all.

The labyris and the lake are two levels of consciousness unequal in skills and power. Yet the lake is part of the creative universe as the Daughter is part of the Mother, and as all women are part of the Goddess. In matriarchy, there are differences between women; all are not equal in wisdom or accomplishments, but each has something to offer for the good of the community. These are spiritual differences; they change as women grow, and they are recognized and accepted. When inner spiritual development is the criteria for position within matriarchy, outer differences have no meaning and they disappear. Inner development changes and grows in every woman as she seeks and learns. The matriarchy values each Sister for her skills and praises her for her attainments. Order in the community, affirmation, correctness and respect, emerge.

MOVEMENT

Nine at the beginning:
    Correct tasks.
    She grows.
The Daughter is not yet fully part of the matriarchy because of her youth and inexperience. In acting simply, she remains free of requirements. If she makes no demands on others, she incurs no debts. She does not yet know her own needs, but floats with the flowing waters.

A woman competent at her tasks is happy to remain a simple Daughter for awhile. She is connected to her roots, and makes progress in spiritual growth. Though she is not yet active in government, she is gaining skills that soon allow her to be. Her work is basic but is positive and correct. She progresses to higher levels and she grows.

Nine in the second position:
    Treading quiet paths.
    The Wisewoman's learning.
    Correctness.
The line speaks of a solitary Wisewoman who chooses retreat from the community. She asks no considerations and has no ambition, only seeks to develop and learn. Her life is calm and even, and by her contentment, she remains free of obligation. She gives what she can of her knowledge and her simplicity benefits all.

Six in the third line:
>   She commits herself
>   Past her skills.
>   She is incorrect.

A woman takes on more than she can complete, and is guilty of folly or recklessness. Such a woman does not succeed without help from her Sisters. By leaving her tasks unfulfilled, she places the matriarchy under greater burdens. Her Sisters finish her work by neglect of their own. The woman loses the respect of her Sisters who depend on her, and matriarchy suffers for her incorrectness.

Nine in the fourth position:
>   She treads on the serpent.
>   Correctness brings no harm.

This is a sensitive action, but the Superior Woman has the power to prevail. She blends certainty with care and correctness, unlike the woman in the third line. She is sure of her goal, and having attempted no more than she can handle, she succeeds.

Nine in the fifth place:
>   Determination,
>   Correctness,
>   And awareness.

This is the hexagram's key line. The Superior Woman is strong and determined. She faces perils but she meets them well. By her correctness, awareness, respect and persistence, she finds in herself what she needs.

Nine at the top:
>   The Superior Woman
>   Acts correctly.
>   Fulfillment.

At completion of her work, the Superior Woman reviews her actions. She has behaved correctly and simply, and has met fulfillment.

11. T'AI / PEACE

Above: K'un — The Pentacle, Earth

Below: Ch'ien — The Labyris, Air

The pentacle and labyris, the earth and universe meet and merge in perfect oneness. "As above, so below"* in abundance, fertility and hope. This is a time of beginnings, the awakening of the Goddess, the first month, February-March, in the Chinese calendar. She is the Chinese New Year, the sabbat Candlemas or Brigid in the Healing Craft, and Powamu in the religion of the Pueblo Indians. She is a time of purification and renewal while the earth prepares for rebirth; a time of lighting candles and relighting the sacred fire to welcome life's return.

In the circle now, new members are named and initiated; in the Kiva children are consecrated to the religious societies. The Southwest Hopi Indians plant hundreds of bean seeds in the Kivas, and the carefully tended sprouts are a reminder and promise of growth.† This is the season of the Crow Mother, the Kachinas; a time of poetry, the arts and muses, and the Triple Goddess. Light appears in the world, the dark recedes. Blessed be.

THE CENTER — Perfect Love and Perfect Trust.

> Peace
> Above and below.
> Perfect harmony.

This is a time when women are at one with the universe. The women partake of the Goddess' light, of her promise, and know that her goodness extends to all living things.

In matriarchy, women blend in harmony. There is consensus without discord. All who are not becoming lovers are certainly Sisters.

*Principle wiccan saying.
†Frank Waters, *Book of the Hopi*, (New York, Ballantine Books, 1963), p. 213-220.

Women walk together in light, in plenty, and in joy. With minds and bodies one, the women are inseparable components of a loving whole. Their faith in matriarchy is blessed and affirmed. Each gives and receives, and knows that she has just begun in fullness.

The harshness of winter gives way to spring, the cold and darkness to warmth and bright awakenings. Women light candles that burn purely white, and offer up poetry and song. They move in grace and goodness in the spiral dance, to a new and brighter dawning. She who draws this hexagram achieves success in her reachings.

REFLECTION

> As above, so below:
> Peace quickens
> Prosperity and love.

The Goddess is one with her women on earth. This is a time of blooming and beginnings, the rebirth of light from darkness. Women are connected to the flow and balance of nature; they grow and wake with her. In matriarchy, she is as the stars.

MOVEMENT

Nine at the beginning:
> Earth at her roots.
> Prosperity.

The Spiritual Woman is as grounded in earth as the roots of the Tree of Life, and she draws others with her. In times of harmony and light, her skills benefit matriarchy by benefiting all. The grounded Spiritual Woman accomplishes much with good fortune. In expressing her own connectedness, she serves.

Nine in the second place:
> She walks in peace.
> Bright blessings.

In brightening times, the Spiritual Woman respects those around her. She offers her skills to the less skilled; she learns from the Mothers and Priestesses. She wastes nothing and finds good use in everything. She is generous and gentle and giving, but knows the time to act or to risk or to take. She cares for all of her Sisters, even those who seem far from her influence. Dissent, force and dominance are things she knows to avoid.

Nine in the third position:
        In enduring
        There is change.
"She changes everything She touches, and everything She touches changes."* Light comes before darkness, winter before spring; all beginnings have ends. The Wheel of the Year, of fortune, turns and none holds her still. In good times, the Spiritual Woman remembers the other side, as in the grey and cold of winter she remembers blooming. With the cycles of the universe before her, she remains connected to her roots. She endures with the strength of her inner nature, and triumphs.

Six in the fourth place:
        All are fulfilled
        In the Mother.
In seasons of promise, women of higher and lesser skills meet on common ground. All are one in the Great Mother. There is no envy or conflict, there is prosperity through peace. Sincerity brings fulfillment to the women of matriarchy; they grow together and are one.

Six in the fifth position:
        The Spiritual Woman
        Gives unselfishly.
In peace, the growth of all skills is harbored. The woman walks in beauty and the sun shines on her skin. She stands tall and feels blessed, and she is. Unafraid of rejection and confident, she learns much and is eager to share in her flowering. The more she gives, the more the Spiritual Woman has within her to give. The matriarchy benefits and the woman attains happiness. Joy comes to all.

Six at the top:
        Change comes
        In her time.
Change comes, but she need not be a setback. After a storm,

---

*Starhawk, *The Spiral Dance: A Rebirth of the Ancient Religion of the Great Goddess*, (San Francisco, Harper and Row Publishers, 1979), p. 67.

darkness gives way to light. By knowledge and acceptance that this is so, the Spiritual Woman weathers all changes, and she waits. Success results from her connectedness; peace, healing and harmony prevail.

12. P'I / DISHARMONY (WANING)

Above: Ch'ien – The Labyris, Air

Below: K'un – The Pentacle, Earth

This hexagram is the duality to Hexagram 11, *Peace*. Instead of a moving together of the earth above and the air below her, the pentacle here is beneath the universe, and is moving away. The powers of labyris creation are not in accord, and waning and darkness result. The symbol represents fall, the Chinese month of August-September, the sabbat Lammas when summer wanes and winter approaches once more. The corresponding Hopi season is the Flute Ceremony, which alternates bi-yearly with the Snake-Antelope ceremonial dances. The harvest is ripening but not yet ready, and the outcome of crops is still uncertain. In wicca, Persephone has left the earth, and the Goddess becomes Demeter, the Reaper.

THE CENTER – The Wheel Turns. A Time to Wait.

Disharmony and waning.
The Spiritual Woman
Waits and
Endures.

Abundance leaves the earth, and earth and universal order are no longer in balance. Peace becomes uncertainty, spring becomes fall, the earth prepares for freezing cold and death. The Goddess of birth

and blooming becomes the Goddess of frosts soon to come. Light
lessens and dark grows in strength. The lesser skilled attempt to lead
the Mothers of matriarchy, and they fail. When the Wheel of Change
turns, all flows once more.

REFLECTION

> Earth and air diverge:
> Disharmony and waning.
> The Spiritual Woman
> Withholds her strength
> And waits.

When disharmony occurs in matriarchy and lesser skilled Sisters
lead, gain and growth decline. The Spiritual Woman acts correctly:
until the forces right themselves and the Wheel turns, she withholds
her support. She does not cause discord or conflict, nor does she enter
conspiracy. She waits.

MOVEMENT

> *Six at the beginning:*
> Earth at her roots.
> Continuing
> Brings gain.

This line is similar to line one of Hexagram 11, but the meaning
is opposed. The Spiritual Woman is pulled away from the life of her
matriarchy by disharmony. She withdraws and she waits. Like a Tree
of Life uprooted, the woman grieves for her connection with the earth.
By continuing in inner spirituality, this interval is short. The matriarchy and her Sisters return to peace, and her worth is valued again.

> *Six in the second line:*
> The Spiritual Woman
> Waits calmly.
> Enduring prevails.

The Spiritual Woman waits until her Sisters listen. She does not
force herself into attention, but accepts the censure of her actions in
good conscience. Her skills are ready for use when they are received.
She bears her suffering and blames none, but knows that her with-

drawal is temporary. She acts correctly for the times.

> *Six in the third position:*
> The lesser skilled women
> Miss their Sister.
> Good fortune.

The lesser skilled women are confused and recognize their Sister's worth. They are unable to meet the needs of matriarchy. They attempt good work, but lack the knowledge that grows with experience. In doing their best, they realize that they have not the skills. For the good of the community, they seek aid.

> *Nine in the fourth place:*
> The Spiritual Woman
> Remains steadfast.
> And is sought.

Disharmony is nearing her change to accord. The Spiritual Woman accepts the work of setting things back into order. Women flock to her for help, and she answers them with her skills. Peace returns in her season.

> *Nine in the fifth position:*
> The Wheel turns,
> Times change.
> The matriarchy benefits.

The Wheel turns; the Spiritual Woman takes action. Peace is not yet accomplished, but is looked for. The Spiritual Woman sees hope in negativity, summer in winter, light in darkness. Change occurs for all. She asks for strength and courage and is aided. That she is aware of danger gives her caution to proceed. Her intentions are good, and her spirituality brings her success.

> *Nine at the top:*
> Disharmony wanes.
> First hesitancy,
> Then achievement.

The Wheel turns, change comes, and the times proceed. The Spiritual Woman acts in harmony with nature. A period of struggle brings about peace, and work is needed to uphold her. Waning in nature is not disharmony and rights herself with the cycle of the year.

Waning in matriarchy is discord to be righted by the Sisters. As fall becomes winter and then spring again, so do women of matriarchy turn waning into new growth. This effort does not come easily. When disharmony ends, all appears still. After the stillness comes motion, achievement and new peace. Hexagram 12, *Disharmony*, becomes Hexagram 11, *Peace*.

13. T'UNG JÊN / SISTERHOOD

Above: Ch'ien — The Labyris, Air

Below: Li — The Wand, Fire

A flaming wand caresses the universe; the element fire is symbol of the brightness of sisterhood. The hexagram is a complement to Hexagram 7, *The Women*, where the women within matriarchy are her strength and source. In *T'ung Jên*, the women are not only the power of the community, but are also the empowerment and love in each other's lives. With clarity and spirituality within and decisiveness without, the Sisters build qualities that make matriarchy possible. They are the union of peaceful women that bonds many into one, the bright torch of woman-energy warming and lighting the earth.

THE CENTER — World Peace Through Sisterhood.

> Proud sisterhood.
> Brightening joy.
> Everything adds to peace.

Sisterhood is a flame, and dances between earth and sky. Enlightened respect and friendship serve the needs of unity in matriarchy. Sisterhood meets in openness, with an attitude of joy. With her comes peace and harmony, and her struggles attain good outcomes. The

Superior Woman is continuing and knowledgeable, clear in her aware-ness of her Sisters and herself. With light and determination, she sees the three-form Goddess all around her. By respect for women, she promotes balance and brightness in her universe.

REFLECTION

> Universal fire:
> Sisterhood in matriarchy.
> The Superior Woman
> Finds order in diversity.

The labyris and the wand of fire move upward, but are not the same. As the universal air expands with accord and order, so do women and the matriarchy illuminate the earth. For sisterhood to attain matriarchy requires balance within the varieties of women's selves, a bonding of energies to one single flame.

MOVEMENT

> *Nine at the beginning:*
> Sisterhood warms.
> She begins.

The warmth of unity begins at the start. The Sisters do not know each other but are open and receptive. No conflicting needs have yet occurred, no opportunities for dissent. Broad ideas are shared by all.

> *Six in the second position:*
> Sisterhood by selection.
> Wrong flaming.

Kali the jealous appears flaming, and the women are tempted by her. She brings disunity and disharmony. Selfishness harms matriarchy and the Sisters within her. By accepting some women selectively, others are left out. Their skills are unrecognized and wasted, and conflict is fostered. To continue this course brings error.

> *Nine in the third place:*
> She lights her skills closely
> And fails.

Sisterhood has cooled to jealousy. The woman watches, envious of her Sisters. She lights her skills in seclusion, hoarding them. She builds a burning gulf inside her that holds her Sisters back. By suspicious thought-forms, the woman creates animosity. By her deeds and attitudes she isolates herself. The longer she remains this way, the more alone she becomes. She uses flame wrongly, and serves only herself.

Nine in the fourth place:
        She looks beyond her fire.
        Some improvement.
The woman comes to her senses. She stands behind her flames and looks beyond. She does not come forward yet, but will. She moves closer towards trust with her Sisters.

Nine in the fifth place:
        Two women.
        Bright blessings.
Two women who are one in heart are alienated. They find each other but they cannot reach to meet. Through actions and obstacles they are drawn together. They work to reconcile differences and eventually reach accord. A spark of greatest warmth unites their efforts. When two women are one within, they do not stay outwardly at odds.

Nine at the top:
        Sisterhood among women.
        Continuing flame.
Beyond the sisterhood of individuals, the Superior Woman seeks to accord herself with her Sisters in matriarchy. She forms relationships that are not as deep as the relationship with her lover. Her sisterhood lights the women near to her daily, but does not warm women she does not know. The unity of all women is not gained, but approaches. She bonds with her lover and is open to her peers; the matriarchy grows stronger. Women reach for each other to the celebration of all, and in time they succeed in reaching all. They move in bright actions and prosperity flames.

14. TA YU / THE GODDESS' GIFTS

Above: Li — The Wand, Fire

Below: Ch'ien — The Labyris, Air

   The universe burns brightly and in her clarity all things are whole. The shortened fifth line dominates this hexagram, but five strength lines work with her in harmony. All things are possible for the Spiritual Woman; she creates abundance and makes her wishes real.

   Women dance around a ritual fire at the summer solstice, Litha, the shortest night of the year. Flames leap to reach the stars and women's voices follow. Light embraces darkness and becomes the grain. Earth matures in fruitfulness and ripening; her bounty is evident and good. The abundance of the universe is the Goddess' gift, and women partake of her welcome.

THE CENTER — Generous Bounty. Warm Actions.

> The Goddess gives
> Of her abundance.
> Blessed be.

   The trigrams symbolize a blending of truth and brightness, the power of circles. Abundance on earth is directed by free will and available to all. Gentleness and clarity draw down the Moon. The time waxes for the Spiritual Woman to achieve. A blazing of courage and strength bring about her goals. Power, the Lady, shows herself in grace. She offers glowing gifts to her Daughters on earth.

REFLECTION

> Light in the Universe:
> The Goddess' gifts.
> The Lady shines below.

The Goddess casts light on earth, on all that lives. The moon in her waxing and waning, shining gentleness and darkness, is a symbol of Goddess. Dark becomes light, winter waxes into summer; the Maiden becomes Mother and Crone. The Spiritual Woman acts in balance with the Lady's changing aspects. By promoting her harmony and brightness, her Eris of humor, and her dark intuition in their places, the Spiritual Woman directs her fate. The Goddess provides all wishes and offers abundance and fullness. The Spiritual Woman uses her gifts well.

MOVEMENT

    Nine at the beginning:
        Harming none,
        She does what she wills.
Gifts carry responsibilities, and the Spiritual Woman has power she uses for good. None are harmed by what she does or thinks. In first recognizing her energies, the Spiritual Woman becomes responsible for their use. What she sends out returns.* Gifts in early beginnings are not yet utilized, and she does neither good nor ill. There are skills to learn and choices to make. By working without harm or manipulation, the Spiritual Woman works well.

    Nine in the second position:
        She begins carefully.
        Warm success.
A skill consists of more than capabilities. She consists of what is done, of what real use the woman makes of her powers. The Mothers and Priestesses help the Spiritual Woman learn; they lend support and offer knowledge. The woman shares her responsibility with Sisters strong enough to help her. By sharing her tasks without exceeding her control, the Spiritual Woman achieves.

    Nine in the third line:
        She offers her skills.
        Full abundance.
A gift is not owned but only channeled. The Spiritual Woman has responsibility to utilize her skills for her Sisters' and her matriar-

---

*Diane Mariechild, *Mother Wit: A Feminist Guide to Psychic Development*, (Trumansburg, NY, The Crossing Press, 1981), p. xiv.

chy's benefit. She shares her blessings and discovers there is always more to give.

Nine in the fourth place:
> She joins with love and trust.
> Open blessings.

The woman joins a circle of Spiritual Women. She meets them in love and trust to learn and to share her gifts. Her skills benefit, she benefits, her circle in matriarchy benefits. All achieve openness, blessings and peace.

Six in the fifth line:
> Connected skills.
> Bright aspects.

The Spiritual Woman uses her gifts wisely, and her Sisters recognize her integrity. Her respect grows for her Sisters, and they in turn respect her. She remains connected to the source of great bounty, and in doing so grows and achieves.

Nine at the top:
> The Goddess' gifts.
> Continuing abundance.

The Spiritual Woman partakes of integrity and dignity, remembering her source of good fortune. She respects her skills and uses them for good. In her fullness of possessions she gives and she receives. She honors the Mothers and Priestesses of matriarchy, honors her Sisters, and honors the Lady who is source of all.

15. CH'IEN / TEMPERANCE

Above: K'un – The Pentacle, Earth

Below: Kên – Keeping Still, Mountain

The trigrams for mountain and earth comprise *Ch'ien*. A mountain reaches towards the universe, and touches the earth and the sky. Her majesty and stillness, her places of trees and wild things, pulse with the life force of the Goddess. The temperance and modesty of the enduring mountain is in harmony with the earth and the universe. Temperance and modesty are still and receptive; they uplift the Superior Woman who practices them.

THE CENTER — The Law of Circles. Affirmation.

> Temperance and order.
> The Superior Woman
> Fulfills her Wheel.

Universal law turns and returns, waxes and wanes. The Superior Woman's fate is determined by her actions, and positive actions fit the Wheel of Life. Change exerts pull on the cosmos and earth, and strives for progress and balance.

The Superior Woman recognizes positive cycles in her life, builds towards them, and acknowledges what destructions are also necessary and good. When her actions do not violate the harmonies, for creation or tearing down, the Superior Woman meets the quality of modesty or temperance. She radiates wisdom at her heights, but has weight and strength at her roots as well. She thus completes her tasks with great certainty, and lives at the center of her Wheel.

REFLECTION

> The pentacle over the mountain:
> Temperance.
> The Superior Woman
> Creates balance.

The base of a mountain extends below the earth and her tip extends above. Her heights and depths are her strength. The Superior Woman works to create order in her life. She balances the distances of high and low and eases conflict, thus bringing peace to her matriarchy.

MOVEMENT

> *Six at the beginning:*
> The Superior Woman
> Proceeds well
> And simply.

A task is easier done without complicating excuses. Promptness and simplicity oil the Wheel. The Superior Woman's good attitude makes her work less difficult. With no complication, there is no resistance or obstacle. The temperate woman completes her work simply and well.

> *Six in the second place:*
> Modesty expressed.
> She continues in
> Positive flow.

The Superior Woman's behavior and attitude show themselves in her actions. Her temperance leads to her triumph, and her effectiveness gains. Continuing brings good outcome in all she attempts.

> *Nine in the third position:*
> The Superior Woman
> Completes her tasks.
> Achievement.

Recognition unbalances the strongest woman, and she is faulted by her Sisters. By remaining modest and temperate, however, the Superior Woman is respected for her achievements. She earns the approval of her Sisters, and completes her work with their help.

> *Six in the fourth line:*
> The temperate woman
> Affirms
> Cosmic order.

All things have their places and times on the Wheel, and temperance avoids excess. The Superior Woman meets her tasks with quiet ability and strives to extend her limits. She recognizes, teaches, and encourages her Sisters' skills as well. The rewards she gains are earned and accepted simply.

Six in the fifth place:
    Temperate actions
    Direct
    Her fate.
Temperance is not passivity. The Superior Woman takes action,
and assumes responsibility for her fate. She does what she can without arrogance, without flaunting her skills or prosperity. She offends
no Sister by her deeds. Temperance appears in attitude and actions;
she does not have to point out her wins.

Six at the top:
    Genuine temperance
    Empowers harmony.
    She prevails.
The Superior Woman shows temperance and modesty in her
actions, and her energy is positive and strong. In conflict, she does
not create dissension or transfer blame to her Sisters. She empowers
balance by her acts and thoughts, and restrains herself to the situation.
By courage and inner strength, she prevails.

A NOTE ON THE LINES
Few hexagrams in the Chinese *I Ching* have six affirming lines.
While this is not the case in Kwan Yin *I Ching*, as the matriarchy
is a positive place, she is still worth noting. The hexagram *Ch'ien*,
translated as temperance or modesty, is a fully favorable hexagram in
traditional translations. Modesty in Chinese thought is considered the
key to all success.

16. YÜ / ENTHUSIASM

Above: Chên – The Awakening, Thunder

Below: K'un – The Pentacle, Earth

The positive fourth line, the one unshortened cast in the hexagram, represents a Mother of matriarchy. The receptive lines are her Sisters, who respond to her with enthusiasm and willingness. The action of the hexagram, thunder meeting the earth, is the spiral of natural order, of cooperation, accord and peace.

Women work willingly to create an orchestra. The Sisters bring skills to play each instrument, and under the direction of a conductor they function as one. In matriarchy too, the Sisters bring individual skills that the Mothers direct to form a whole.

THE CENTER — Willing Cooperation. Golden Peace.

> Enthusiasm and
> Willingness.
> The Mothers find
> Many helpers.

The Mothers are connected to the needs of women in matriarchy, and are connected to cycles of the universe and earth. They find receptivity and cooperation among the Sisters they serve, and gain helpers. Every woman in the community participates and offers skills, and many hands make light work. There is fulfillment in the matriarchy's undertakings, since the Sisters are willing in their tasks and their decisions are made by consensus and choice. Enthusiasm binds and promotes peace where power-over does not exist; good outcomes greet willing endeavors.

REFLECTION

> Thunder awakens the earth:
> An image of willingness.
> Music of the spheres.

A summer storm brings rain to the earth, a release of heat and stress. The women are renewed, and take time to celebrate and make music. Some dance with enthusiasm while their Sisters play drums and flutes. They are drawn together in willingness as a group.

Music mirrors the song of the universe and the Goddess. She is joyous and powerful, an act of pleasure that is one of the rituals. Spirituality unites with women's joy; the universe and earth meet in ecstasy and in harmony become one.

MOVEMENT

> *Six in the first line:*
> Over enthusiasm.
> She errs.

Over enthusiasm, arrogance, is power-over that the Superior Woman avoids, but willing enthusiasm is a virtue. Enthusiasm is not used to draw attention to oneself, nor is based on personal reward. Good actions reflect beyond boasted words: cooperation and willingness are qualities that benefit all.

> *Six in the second place:*
> Centered willingness.
> She continues well.

The Superior Woman is not deluded by enthusiastic words, but relies on actions and her inner sense. She does not fawn or withhold honest praise, but is steady, open and secure. In times of conflict, the Superior Woman withdraws; she analyzes outcomes before she speaks. She is centered and knows when to use her willingness. For the good of her matriarchy, she knows when to wait and to act.

> *Six in the third position:*
> She looks to the Mothers
> And cooperates.

Line two is initiative and responsibility; here, willingness involves deferring. The Superior Woman, in enthusiasm to help her Sisters, learns where her skills are needed. By placing herself where she is strongest, though she may not want to be there, the Superior Woman cooperates and does the most good. To hesitate in responding to direction brings error. Deferring to the Mothers' wisdoms is correct.

> *Nine in the fourth place:*
> Sincere willingness.
> Enthusiastic efforts.

By her strength and certainty, the Superior Woman gains willingness from others. Her Sisters follow her in confidence and calm. By her respect for their enthusiasm and skills, she wins their wholehearted efforts.

Six in the fifth line:
    Stress hinders
    Her achievements.

The Superior Woman under stress is unable to cooperate with others. She has no enthusiasm for activities and no joy. By grounding herself to release tension, by sharing responsibilities with her Sisters, she lessens the strain in her life and is able to act more willingly.

Six at the top:
    Enthusiastic awakening.
    No error.

The Superior Woman avoids excessive enthusiasm, but if she errs she changes her ways. Her Sisters help and support her in her growth. By recognition and awareness, she transforms arrogance into cooperation and harmony. Awakened self-knowledge is positive gain.

17. SUI / FOLLOWING

Above: Tui — The Joyous Daughter, Lake

Below: Chên — The Awakening, Thunder

Tui, the Joyous Daughter rises over *Chên*, Awakening, and Joy over movement means to follow. The young Daughter, following her Mothers' wisdoms gladly, is awakened to her own strengths. She follows before she leads, and learns to flow with situations and occasions by her Mothers' examples. In serving the Daughter grows, and her Sisters choose to follow her. As she gains in skills and wisdoms, she becomes the Superior Woman and a Mother of matriarchy.

© Robin Wood 1987

THE CENTER — Following In Her Time. She Learns and Leads.

> She who follows
> Learns to lead.
> Continuing flow.

By continuing in the positive and good, the Superior Woman grows in her skills. She follows her Mothers and Sisters and learns from them, and she who follows is followed in turn. "One thing becomes another"* is the Goddess' law, and only under this principle does following or leading take place in balance. With sensitivity to correctness, the Superior Woman meets her goals. She flows to the needs of her moment, to her range of abilities, and to the input of Sisters around her.

REFLECTION

> Thunder on the lake:
> Following.
> The Superior Woman
> Grows with her Wheel.

In fall, the life force leaves the earth and is hidden until spring; thunder on the lake is waiting energy. Following mirrors the Wheel of Life as an acceptance and flowing within time. The Superior Woman, who has worked hard for matriarchy in her years, allows herself more space for inactivity as she becomes a Crone. Her choice is positive because she recognizes cosmic cycles and flows with them. She passes her cares to younger Sisters, but remains to teach and advise. Her position in matriarchy is not lessened, but is changed. The Superior Woman does not work against the force of nature, she follows her. She serves the matriarchy as she may.

MOVEMENT

> *Nine at the beginning:*
> Times follow and flow.
> Continuing success.

Starhawk, The Spiral Dance: A Rebirth of the Ancient Religion of the Great Goddess, (San Francisco, Harper and Row Publishers, 1979), p. 9.

She who leads follows, and the follower leads; the Daughter follows the Mothers and becomes a Mother herself. She is sure in her principles and spirituality, and is there to teach as well as to learn. The Superior Woman is open to her Sisters and Mothers, to her Daughters and herself. She is a worker in matriarchy, and does not reject Sisters whose ideas are not her own. She flows with all and listens to all; she excludes none. In matriarchy, all women are equal; none is above or below.

Six in the second line:
    She follows
    The child within.
The Superior Woman is an adult but follows the child within her. Each woman is a Mother and a Daughter. In touch with her child self, she does not lose touch with joy. Her connection with her beginnings serves her well.

Six in the third place:
    Following she leads.
    Continuing joy.
The Superior Woman follows her Sisters and her inner self. She learns from her Mothers and teaches Sisters less experienced. She connects to all women in matriarchy and to cycles of the Goddess, and sees divinity in herself and in all. Her Sisters recognize her worth; her continuing and joy bring harmony. By following, she finds that she leads.

Nine in the fourth position:
    Her Sisters follow her.
    No hesitation.
As her skills gain respect and her Sisters follow her, the Superior Woman remains connected to her roots. She recognizes and resists manipulation, and does not take advantage of others. By focusing her goals on peace and correctness in matriarchy, on progress and good actions, the Superior Woman gains truth and self-determination. Without self-serving and egotism, she need not hesitate when her Sisters follow her.

Nine in the fifth place:
    Great integrity.
    She achieves.

The Goddess as thought-form is the harmony of earth in all women. By setting her sights on the peace and perfection of the Lady, the Superior Woman gains integrity and endurance to achieve.

Six at the top:
    The Wisewoman
    Leaves isolation.
A respected Wisewoman, a healer withdrawn from the community, is approached by a follower. The Daughter asks the Wisewoman for help, and she returns to the matriarchy to share her skills. There remains a bond between the Wisewoman and the Daughter who approached her. The Daughter leads the teacher, and the Wisewoman leads in her turn. Both Sisters flow with their times, are followers and leaders, and are blessed in the turning of the Wheel.

18. KU / DECAY

— —
— —   *Above*: Kên — Keeping Still, Mountain
— —

———
———   *Below*: Sun — The Gentle Wind/Wood
— —

Ku is a fallen tree trunk; insects destroy her in the symbol of decay. The softness of wood meets the obstinate hardness of the mountain, and decay and destruction of the wood result. There is a feeling here that something needful is not done, but decay is also, in her place and time, a natural and necessary phenomenon. The tree spoils and her wood becomes part of the land; matter changes form but is not destroyed. Decay is an aspect of the balance of the universe; her presence is the need for change.

THE CENTER — Actions Determine Fate. Choice and Energy Prevail.

> Action against decay.
> Women's energy.
> By effort she prevails.

Endings are followed by beginnings in the universal cycle, destructions by creations, and the Spiritual Woman determines her own fate within them. Action in good measure reverses decay by effort, risk and strategy. She acts forcefully, but thinks clearly of consequences before she does.

The Spiritual Woman understands decay before she attempts to reverse her. Softness and yielding give way to woman's strength and empowerment; endings and destructions are new starts.

REFLECTION

> Wood below the mountain:
> Image of decay.
> The Spiritual Woman
> Motivates her Sisters.

The Spiritual Woman draws her Sisters' attentions to issues and leads the matriarchy to right wrongs. In courage and gentleness she energizes and motivates her Sisters. The hardness of the mountain and softness of wood reverse to result in change.

MOVEMENT

> *Six at the beginning:*
> Righting wrongs.
> Perils yield to triumph.

The traditional order has decayed, but women are not lost; matriarchy is the remedy of their futures. The old order changes to a fresh and strong new day. The Sisters are excited and aroused to take charge. From decay, stagnation and danger come rebirth, rebuilding, triumph and success.

Nine in the second position:
>Changing things.
>She knows when to wait.

Softness results in spoilage, but gentle redress is required. The Spiritual Woman acts thoughtfully to create change. She avoids confusion and conflict among her Sisters, and knowing when to move she moves carefully.

Nine in the third place:
>Reversing the past.
>Some nostalgia.

The Spiritual Woman moves too quickly in attempting change. Small hindrances arise that hang to her cloak and pull her down, but more in this case is less harmful than not enough. The Spiritual Woman grows impatient. Her energy is required to effect changes, and changes are greatly needed. By shaking her cloak and continuing, she does no wrong.

Six in the fourth line:
>Turning the cheek.
>Regretful continuing.

The times require change but the woman refuses to act. By turning away she assures failure, and continuing in decay brings regrets. In a time of action, the Spiritual Woman takes charge.

Six in the fifth place:
>Taking action.
>Establishing success.

The Spiritual Woman recognizes decay from older times. She sees the need of changes and is willing but unable to act. With the help of her Sisters in matriarchy, energy is pooled and decay is reversed. They rescue as much as they can.

Nine at the top:
>She withdraws
>But serves well.

A few women in matriarchy choose the paths of a Mother. Not everyone has wish or skill to govern, and the choice of other roads is praised. Some Sisters are strongest in inner skills, in spiritual development, and withdraw for a time to learn. They become Priestesses,

Wisewomen, healers and teachers. That they do not act directly against decay in society, does not mean they ignore her. Each woman has skills and her skills all have uses. The Priestess does not criticize the Mothers; her obligation is to work with them for the matriarchy's stability and good. By withdrawing from government, the Spiritual Woman creates the inner values she teaches to her Sisters. In this way she combats decay and contributes far reaching good.

19. LIN / APPROACH

Above: K'un — The Pentacle, Earth

Below: Tui — The Joyous Daughter, Lake

Lin is the promise of approaching fullness, the year's waxing towards spring. The Chinese twelfth month, January-February is represented here; she is Brigid in the wiccan calendar, and Pamuya and the Kachina Dances in Hopi cosmology. These symbol systems are connected in meaning. This is the after-peak of winter, the time when cold begins to break, when the promise of spring approaches on earth. Days grow longer and light returns, the candles are relit; ewes and mares are heavy with coming births. By the positioning of the tri-grams, the gladness of the lake rises to meet a waiting earth.

In matriarchy, approach is a favorable starting of efforts. Now is the time to begin a love affair, to take on a new creative project. The Mothers smile and are eager to teach the Daughters, and matriarchy begins a new expansion. The Goddess wakes from winter sleep to bring newness to the world. Now is the time to begin — there is no need to wait.

THE CENTER — A Time of Waxing. New Births.

> A time of approach
> And new births.
> Effort furthers
> Till she changes.

Beginnings are favorable and triumph comes with effort and action. Good use is made of the waxing of the year. Although the beans of Powamu sprout green in the Kivas and the candles are relit in the circles, the year continues to change. In the fullness of time, the light that approaches withdraws again. Within all beginnings are endings, within all approaches retreats: the Superior Woman in spring-time moves towards her hopes and her goals.

REFLECTION

> A lake meets the earth;
> Approach and begin.
> Time and boundless
> Opportunity.

The Goddess is the earth that meets the joyous lake; the lake is water and water sustains all life. The Mother shares her bounty with her Daughter; the Daughter becomes a Mother herself: this is the web of harmony and order. Winter's barrenness changes to spring, and the rebirthing Goddess is the rebirth of all. The earth approaching is a time of growth in women's lives. Possibilities are boundless; the Superior Woman makes of them what she will.

MOVEMENT

Nine at the beginning:
> They approach
> Beginning efforts.

Energy manifests and is received; the Superior Woman approaches her Sisters. In matriarchy, there are new beginnings; among lovers new affairs. The Superior Woman chooses correctly and without excess. The time is right, and by acting with determination, she finds gain.

Nine in the second place:
> Approach together,
> Good starts.

The Superior Woman knows the time is now. She makes her move with confidence and. is welcomed. Change proceeds on the Wheel, but not before her time, and she need not fear reversals yet. Sisters find each other, lovers meet in spring; life offers good abundance when two approach as one.

Six in the third position:
> She takes approach
> For granted.

The Superior Woman gains influence and her energy rises; approach is in her hands. She does not take her power for granted in actions or words. The Sister she approaches warns the Superior Woman that she errs. If she heeds and changes attitude, she takes no loss.

Six in the fourth line:
> Successful approach.
> No error.

She opens herself to the Sister she approaches. They become lovers who were first friends. Energy is high and rising; they become one in understanding, become one. In the honest beginnings of a mutual love, there can be no error.

Six in the fifth position:
> A Mother approaches
> Her matriarchy.

A Mother comes to her matriarchy with a project, and by consensus her Sisters agree. In mutual sharing of skills and respect the project begins. The Mother approaches her Sisters for help and they approach her with willingness. She listens to their ideas and uses their knowledge for the good of all. The Superior Woman begins from her own roots, then approaches her Sisters and triumphs.

Six at the top:
> A Wisewoman approaches.
> Bright blessings.

A Wisewoman chooses to return to matriarchy for a time. She approaches her Sisters, approaches her community and is welcomed.

She brings blessings to Sisters she chooses to teach, and brings benefit and comfort to Sisters she heals. In her actions she earns respect, and by her approach the matriarchy strengthens.

20. KUAN / CONTEMPLATION (EXAMPLE)

Above: Sun — The Gentle Wind/Wood

Below: K'un — The Pentacle, Earth

Kuan is the Spiritual Woman who contemplates the Mysteries of the Goddess and the Wheel of Life, and is an example by this to her matriarchy. The season is late fall, the Chinese tenth month of November-December.* These are months of dwindling light, the descent of earth into winter darkness. *Kuan* is the time of the Crone, of Demeter refusing life while Persephone is gone. Samhain is past, the night when the dead and unborn touch the presently living, and when Hopi Kachinas leave earth for the underworld. In the death and end of the year lie the seeds of her new beginnings; the Spiritual Woman contemplates the cycle.

THE CENTER — She Contemplates the Mysteries. Blessings.

> Contemplation:
> Demeter's sacrifice.
> Perfect trust.

November and December are darkening months. The earth bows to the Goddess as Reaper, and her sacrifice assures rebirth. The old year dies after harvest; the fields are cold and still. Persephone roams the underworld, the the gates of death are open. Though darkness

---

*Richard Wilhelm and Cary F. Baynes set this hexagram at the eighth rather than the tenth month.

dominates awhile, Persephone returns to Demeter with spring, the Kachinas return to the Pueblos, and life rebegins.

The Spiritual Woman's contemplation of the Mysteries is her most perfect trust. Out of darkness comes light, and out of light darkness. The effects of contemplation on the Spiritual Woman's life mirrors the changes of the earth herself. Her peace is evident, and her Sisters and Daughters follow her example.

REFLECTION

> Wind caressing earth:
> Contemplation.
> Persephone chooses life.

The gentle wind caresses the earth; she is change, and tosses all before her. Persephone dwells in the underworld, as Demeter rages and mourns. The earth transforms and all life dies.

A woman shapes a bowl of clay and sets her in the air to dry. By action of the gentle wind, the earth hardens, and clay is transformed to pottery. In matriarchy too, the Spiritual Woman changes herself by contemplation and is an example to all.

MOVEMENT

> Six in the beginning:
> Childish understanding.
> In a child, no error.

A Daughter looks at the Mysteries, but does not understand. She lives within the spiral all the same. In a Daughter, lack of depth reflects her lack of experience. She learns what she can, and as she grows she gains in thought. The Mothers protect her and she comes to no harm.

The Spiritual Woman, however, has grown in knowledge. She understands her existence at the core of the Wheel, and exists at the center of matriarchy as well. Her example to the Daughter is the best she has to give.

> Six in the second position:
> Outward contemplation.
> She continues.

The woman who sees only herself has restricted her vision, and does not understand her Sisters. This is a stage of development through which some Daughters pass. The Spiritual Woman widens her viewpoint before she influences others. Through continuing contemplation her example grows.

Six in the third line:
>Living contemplation.
>She chooses.

The Daughter transforms to a Spiritual Woman. She understands the inner qualities of her life and relates them to the universe; she places herself in the feelings of her Sisters. She learns compassion and devotion to the Mysteries and approaches the Priestesses to learn more. Her outlook has changed. By accepting superior examples, the Daughter becomes an example herself. She opens to contemplation and does not remain in the dark.

Six in the fourth position:
>Contemplation of matriarchy.
>She becomes an example.

The Spiritual Woman is connected to the spiral and the matriarchy, and knows the universe mirrors the earth. Her inner strength and transformation radiate from her being. She influences her Sisters, teaches her Daughters, and becomes an example to follow.

Nine in the fifth place:
>Self-contemplation.
>No error.

The Spiritual Woman is self-aware, and knows the influence of her example. When her actions and attitude are good, her matriarchy benefits and she achieves. By continuing on inner paths, by contemplation of the Mysteries and her part in them, the Spiritual Woman helps matriarchy and herself.

Nine at the top:
>Contemplation of infinity.
>Bright blessings.

A Wisewoman contemplates the Mysteries, and by her example and knowledge she helps her matriarchy grow. In time she shares her learning, but chooses solitude for now. In the example of her scholarship, she works for the good of all.

21. SHIH HO / TAKING HOLD (RECOURSE)

Above: Li — The Wand, Fire

Below: Chên — The Awakening, Thunder

The trigrams are the lightning and thunder of a storm. An important hexagram, *Shih Ho* encompasses all four elements; she is a storm that cleanses the earth and air by water and fire. Lightning strikes, and thunder rolls across the sky; rain follows. Tension is released and the earth is refreshed and renewed.

In matriarchy, conflict between Sisters is changed to accord, and consensus is the thunderstorm of the process. By clearing the air and releasing energies and angers, new awarenesses are made. The Sisters take hold of their differences and resolve them in peaceful recourse.

THE CENTER — Taking Hold of Conflict. Resolution is Recourse.

> Taking hold brings recourse.
> Resolution of conflict.
> Consensus clears the air.

When conflict arises in matriarchy, consensus or mediation resolves her. A woman of blocked energies disturbs the bond of the group. The Sisters work by consensus to open her channels; they offer her energy and love and make her feel wanted and welcome. If this is not enough, a mediator is named and the woman or opposing women work the issue through. No deliberate hurt is administered or received, no punishment or retribution is involved. The change is to peace and unity, and the process is matriarchy's strength.

REFLECTION

> A thunderstorm:
> Taking hold and recourse.
> The Mothers resolve differences.

Resolution is superior to punishment, for she leads to accord and power within. Matriarchy sets standards by consensus, and resolves problems by consensus and mediation. The Sisters are the process of governing, and they lessen the need for recourse. By combination of fire's light and thunder's transformations, renewal refreshes the earth. The light of consensus and the transformations of mediation renew the matriarchy. By taking hold of these forms of leadership, conflict is resolved to peace.

MOVEMENT

> *Nine at the beginning:*
> Her Sisters speak
> To her in circle.

The Sisters approach her in circle to say what is troubling them. The woman is shown her error, how her fault appears. She is treated gently and not censured; her fault is small and within her awareness to correct. There is no blame on the woman or her Sisters. With light, accord is reached.

> *Six in the second line:*
> There is no resolve.
> She takes hold of conflict.

The woman in this line is unable to resolve conflict with her Sisters. The meeting is focused on helping her, but she refuses or is unable to understand. The woman grows stubborn and her Sisters less patient; implementation of consensus begins. Light is not clarity and thunder is heard. A conflict in matriarchy hurts all.

> *Six in the third place:*
> A mediator shows blockage.
> The woman is partly awakened.

If consensus fails to heal conflict, a mediator is named. The woman's block is revealed to her and she becomes defensive, but light is a step in the right direction. New awareness brings change, though the process is painful. There is no error here, but the outcome is still uncertain. Renewal awakens from the storm.

Nine in the fourth position:
   Powerful emotions.
   Endurance brings accord.
The process of opening up is difficult; there are great and powerful emotions. Only by taking hold firmly and with determination is the matter resolved. The Sisters apply consensus and mediation; they are gentle and aware, but strong in their principles. The woman awakens to understanding; she is hurt but endures. Taking hold is gained through gentleness and strength.

Six in the fifth line:
   She is aware of dangers,
   And learns the middle road.
Matters of conflict are not easy to resolve, however clear the issue seems. A Sister who engages in conflict does not wish to sow discord, and her situation is a delicate one. She is embraced and reassured, but is also made aware. With her Sister's help, she learns the middle road, the road of life, and with patience and continuing there is change.

Nine at the top:
   Unresolved conflict.
   Misfortune.
In a situation where consensus and mediation fail, and the women are not brought into accord, misfortune results. The negativity of one Sister effects all. Every effort is made to gain peace.

22. PI / GRACE

Above: Kên – Keeping Still, Mountain

Below: Li – The Wand, Fire

Pi is a volcano under the mountain. Her glow rises up towards the peak, caressing her with light and grace. Grace is the element that makes a relationship or object special. She is accord and harmony, the pleasing of perfections and minds, the oneness of function and form.

A structure is raised by women's hands. Through planning, effort and skill, foundations are laid and walls rise. The structure becomes a home, a place of safety and beauty. Form and function — aesthetics, accomplishment and usefulness — are aspects of grace. The structure of matriarchy is built this way, as well.

THE CENTER — Perfection and Grace. Rare blessings.

> Grace is perfection
> And beauty.
> A rare blessing.

Grace is a quality not to be taken for granted. She is gentleness and unifying form. There is strength in grace, as there is strength in the overlying mountain, and strength is prime in this reading. The fire below the mountain, the reflection of the inner glow of the volcano, is the gentle and softening aspect of this hexagram. In matriarchy, grace is the circle of a Hopi bowl, the power of a healing ritual, the warmth of loom-woven cloth. Aesthetics are traditions interpreted in an artist's hands; by understanding harmonies in the universe, women recreate them on earth. Her harmonies are the graces that shape women's lives.

The light of deep meditation is also grace, clarity within and strength without.* She is the plane of thought and artistic creation, the beauty of crystalline ideals. Through meditation on perfection, women bring her into reach.

REFLECTION

> The wand under the mountain:
> An image of grace.
> Beauty in all
> She touches.

---

*Richard Wilhelm and Cary F. Baynes, Trans., *The I Ching or Book of Changes*, Bollingen Series XIX, (Princton, NJ, Princeton University Press, 1950 and 1967), p. 91n.

Glowing light touches a mountain and makes her strength beautiful. The wand of grace shines deeply in the life force. Her harmony in daily living makes the ordinary special; there is beauty in all she touches, all she is.

MOVEMENT

Nine at the beginning:
    She walks in beauty
    And in grace.
There is grace in the beauty of a woman's body — in her movement, her form, her shape, her breasts and her skin. She is perfection, and a part of the Goddess and the earth.

Six in the second place:
    Beauty of form
    And function.
The beauty of a well-made cooking pot or length of woven cloth reflects the harmony of the universe. When what she does is done well, however lowly the object or task, the Superior Woman participates in grace. She brightens the matriarchy with her efforts.

Nine in the third position:
    Participation in grace.
    She gives and receives.
Grace is a challenge to the Superior Woman. She participates in beauty in all things, and in beauty she gives and she takes. Continuing flow succeeds.

Six in the fourth line:
    Simple graces.
    Joyful choosing.
Simplicity and peace flow from within. The Superior Woman finds beauty in her lover, in everything she is and does, and they are one in grace. Blessings transcend all space and time. The choosing and finding are joyous when two women meet in love.

Six in the fifth place:
    Grace in the earth.
    She seeks the land.

A woman withdraws from the cares of matriarchy to return to the land. She seeks elemental simplicity and the grace of the Goddess, and finds them in all she sees. The Superior Woman meets a woman or a land she can love. She offers what she can in openness. Her sincerity brings success and the love of the graceful earth.

> *Nine at the top:*
> Perfect grace
> Is simplicity.

Grace reveals function and harmony; perfection is in substance and in all she is. The Superior Woman recognizes grace in her lover, in the earth, in matriarchy, in the Goddess — and she seeks her in art and in her life.

23. PO / SPLITTING APART

Above: Kên — Keeping Still, Mountain

Below: K'un — The Pentacle, Earth

The trigrams show a mountain weakened by cracks in the earth: even the strength of mountains meets failure under overwhelming stress. The lines picture a tower, the roof of which (the long top line) is about to fall. In the Chinese, the five shortened lines are the triumph of the patient earth over the unyielding of a mountain. *Po* is great transformations, a splitting apart.

The hexagram involves the ninth Chinese month of October-November, the zodiac sign of Scorpio. She is Samhain, the New Year in the wiccan calendar, and Wuwuchim, the New Year and emergence of the Hopi creation cycle. Both represent time's death and rebirth, the beginnings within the ends. In the splitting apart of an old cycle, a new one is born; from death emerges life in the turning Wheel. Like

the Tower card in the Tarot, destructions are not deaths but transformations. A circle has no end.

THE CENTER — Endings and Beginnings. A Time to Wait.

> Splitting apart.
> Waiting.
> Do not move.

Endings come, and from endings emerge new starts. Changes
are at hand: the Superior Woman waits.

The trigrams suggest correct action. The pentacle of earth is
beneath the stillness of the mountain. The Superior Woman submits
to change, accepts the endings that come, and waits for her new cycles.
These conditions are part of the spiral, the Wheel of Life. Action
now does not achieve.

REFLECTION

> A mountain on earth:
> Splitting apart.
> Endings rebegin at
> The center of the Wheel.

When a mountain or tower stands solidly, there is no error. When
her foundations are not strong, however, collapse and change are inevitable.

In matriarchy, earth supports all, and her Sisters are the earth
sustaining the mountain. When change comes to women, change
comes to matriarchy as well. In splitting apart comes ending, and from
ending comes the new. When a time of change is completed, the tower
of matriarchy is secure again, as a mountain standing on solid ground.

MOVEMENT

> *Six at the beginning:*
> Conflict undermines.
> The Superior Woman waits.

Conflict among Sisters causes splitting apart in matriarchy, and
brings about misfortune for all. The circumstance holds danger, but

nothing helps at this time. The Superior Woman waits for her time of action.

> *Six in the second line:*
> Conflict continues.
> She still waits.

The power of conflict and peril gains. Trouble increases with no resolution in sight, no help or healing touch. Extreme sensitivity is vital. The Superior Woman waits for her opportunity in a time of splitting apart. She lessens the stresses on herself and her matriarchy by stepping back temporarily.

> *Six in the third position:*
> Reluctant splitting apart.
> No recourse.

The Superior Woman enters conflict, but not by her own choice. She is swept away by the status of her time. Through inner awareness, and the help of a Mother in matriarchy whose knowledge she seeks, she finds the clarity to withdraw from dissent. She opposes her Sisters, but resistance in this way is not error. She withstands splitting apart.

> *Six in the fourth place:*
> Splitting apart.
> Misfortune.

The situation is at crisis, and is the moment of disaster for matriarchy and her women. She is the time after waiting and before action, the moment of shock and trauma. Splitting apart reaches the mountaintop, and plunges to the depths of the earth below.

> *Six in the fifth line:*
> The cycle changes.
> Waiting is fulfilled.

The law of darkness, the earth principle, is transformed. She is no longer in conflict, as change occurs. Splitting apart submits to accordance, mediation and resolution. The Wheel of Change turns, ending reverts to beginning, conflict resolves to peace From the bottom, she goes upward. Actions further, and waiting is fulfilled.

> *Nine at the top:*
> Splitting ends
> In new beginnings.

At destruction's end, new beginnings emerge. The Superior Woman is heeded by her Sisters in matriarchy again. Now is the time to rebuild, and in rebuilding the matriarchy grows stronger than before. Destruction destroys destruction, and with her collapse the splitting apart ends.

24. FU / THE WHEEL OF LIFE (RETURN)

Above: K'un — The Pentacle, Earth

Below: Chên — The Awakening, Thunder

A positive line pushes upward and the shortened lines above her turn with the motion of the Wheel, the Wheel of fortune, chance or life. This hexagram is concurrent with the Eleventh Chinese month, that of December-January, the winter solstice. She is the sabbat Yule, the longest night, after which the light returns. In the Hopi calendar she is Soyál, and in astrology the sign of Capricorn. A time of rest and darkness before life is reawakened, she is the point of zenith, the instant before birth. In the Tarot, this hexagram is connected to The Wheel of Fortune, a major arcana card.

The Wheel of Life is a circle of returnings. Where Hexagram 23, *Po* is Samhain and endings, *Fu* precedes rebirth and emergence. She is the timeless instant before action, the moment before the newborn's first cry. She is the center of the Wheel, who is the Wheel herself. In the Kiva there is silence, fasting and deep meditation. From the core and height of darkness comes new light.*

In Tarot, The Wheel of Fortune is the zodiac, the wiccan Wheel of the Year, the Hopi Road of Life. To draw her, or this hexagram in a reading means that something 'fortunate' is about to happen.† After

---

*Frank Waters, *Book of the Hopi*, (New York, Ballantine Books, 1963), p. 188.
†Vicki Noble, *Motherpeace: A Way to the Goddess Through Myth, Art and Tarot*, (San Francisco, Harper and Row Publishers, 1983), p. 88.

darkness, the year swings upward in her orbit; the Goddess is reborn.

THE CENTER — She Rebegins. Bright Turnings.

> The Wheel of Life.
> Process and Changes.
> Bright turnings.

Yule is the longest night of the year, December 22, the winter solstice. After this night, days lengthen and light gradually returns; from winter's darkest peak emerges spring. The Wheel of Life is transformation in natural ways. Through peaceful growth and process, the old becomes new.

The Wheel of Life is the Goddess and the earth herself, and all things occur in her time and place. Change proceeds on earth, in women's lives and in matriarchy with natural accord. Balance is maintained and conflict does not arise; life continues on her cyclic path of endings and returns. Good fortune is in reach of all.

REFLECTION

> Awakening below earth:
> Life returning.
> A moment's pause.

The Solstice in China, in western wicca and in the Kiva is a time of motionless waiting, of bated breath and pause. She is the newborn year of all potential. The earth awaits awakening by the life force within her, but her energy is still in the underworld. Life begins slowly and change is not yet felt or seen.

All forms of return are symbolized in this hexagram: the return to peace after discord, love after isolation, wholeness after pain. New beginnings are nurtured and protected to grow strong.

MOVEMENT

> *Nine at the beginning:*
> Small divergence,
> Small return.
> A Sister diverges from matriarchy's path of life in a minor way.

She realizes her error, is enlightened, and returns. In her inner growth she achieves a small clarity, a small gain towards balance and peace.

> *Six in the second place:*
> She chooses return.
> Blessings.

Choice and will are involved in all returnings. The Superior Woman is centered in the Wheel of Life that she travels with her Sisters. In personal matters, she separates her road from others, but in matters of matriarchy they return as one.

> *Six in the third position:*
> She returns to ask
> And is protected.

A Daughter seeks her place on the Wheel. She chooses a thought and then changes her mind. Life transforms more quickly than she understands. She returns to ask the Mothers again and again. In her newness, the Mothers protect and nurture her, but give her room to learn. By her reachings and returnings, she grows within the Wheel.

> *Six in the fourth line:*
> Together
> They return.

The Superior Woman walks with her Sisters in matriarchy, and she does so in accord and peace. She meets a lover, and they travel together from then on. The women, choosing good actions in the community and in relationships, return in blessings and joy.

> *Six in the fifth line:*
> Return in time.
> Continuing flow.

At a time of returning, the Superior Woman seeks self-awareness. She attempts to analyze past actions, their consequences in her life and in her matriarchy. She acknowledges her strengths and weaknesses and takes awareness on her further roads. For this there is success.

> *Six at the top:*
> Losing the Wheel.
> Wrong returning.

The Superior Woman mistakes the road and loses her time for

returning. Realizing her error, she seeks correct paths to regain the Wheel. With her return to connectedness and matriarchy, she gains benefit for herself and all.

25. WU WANG / INNOCENCE (WONDER)

—————
—————   *Above:* Ch'ien — The Labyris, Air
—————

—— ——
—— ——   *Below:* Chên — The Awakening, Thunder
—————

The hexagram is the balance of nature found on the earth and in grounded and connected women. Awakening action is below the trigram for the labyris universe. Motion under the labyris is the Wheel of Life, her harmony and primal innocence. What is natural is often wondrous, and surprise and wonder are aspects of this hexagram.

A woman plants a seed: from first a tiny sprout, a strong vine grows. On the vine are delicate flowers that draw bees. The bees create honey, and the flowers become small fruit. The fruit matures and is pleasing to the taste, and honey and fruit nourish the woman that planted the seed. Within the eaten fruit are seeds to plant again, to continue the cycle and wonder of life.

THE CENTER — Continuing Wonder. Peace.

> Innocence:
> In the life force,
> Wonder and balance.

A woman is part of the Goddess who is the earth, and who guides all actions. Connection with immanence brings the Superior Woman into harmony, into balance and power from within; she achieves inner certainty and empowerment. Not all that is natural and primal, however, is made of light; there are dark forces to the Goddess' Moon as well. With spirituality and correctness, the Superior Woman remains centered and grounded in the Universe, in her light and dark. She partakes of the power and wonder of the earth and stars.

REFLECTION

> The awakening universe:
> Innocence, wonder
> And immanence.

The thunder life force awakens in spring and creation begins in the universe. Light and warmth return, plants appear and grow green, young animals and Daughters are born. All reflect in their awakening the rebirth of the Goddess, of the earth in primal innocence. A woman of matriarchy mirrors the earth; the land and all living around her emerge new. The Superior Woman learns wonders; she nurtures and blesses all life.

MOVEMENT

> *Nine at the beginning:*
> A Daughter's innocence.
> Gentle awakening.

The Daughter follows her caprices with wonder, and her world is as new as she is. Everything she sees surprises her, and she learns from all she meets. The Mothers protect a Daughter from harm, but teach her and encourage her to expand and explore. In her open and gentle innocence, the Daughter is one with the earth.

> *Six in the second line:*
> Every act in her time.
> Natural flowing.

The Superior Woman does not expect fruit at blossom time. She takes the bounty of each season as she comes, and lives in the here and now. Each task has a time and place in the cycle of life, a goodness in herself. Orchards bloom and bear in natural season; the Superior Woman nurtures her flow.

> *Six in the third place:*
> Time's innocence.
> She changes.

Spring emerges from winter, and the Wheel changes for all, Within the natural cycle, within innocence, the Superior Woman is aware and part of time. She proceeds on the Wheel of Life and the universe; from Daughter to Mother to Wisewoman, Maiden to Mother to Crone, she travels each turn of her road.

Nine in the fourth position:
    Inner integrity.
    Innocent peace.

The Superior Woman knows that inner growth is not lost or taken away. She is grounded and at peace in this knowledge, and works toward spiritual gain. By trust in herself and in her matriarchy and the Goddess, her innocence is assured. She achieves new heights of success.

Nine in the fifth place:
    Self-healing.
    Wonder furthers.

An illness or imbalance from within is treated and healed from within. The Superior Woman seeks self-awareness for her cures, and by healing herself she heals a portion of the earth. She grows strong and vital with empowerment, and her innocence and wonder are part of her natural universe.

Nine at the top:
    Simplistic innocence.
    She waits.

The Superior Woman learns when to wait; she creates failure by acting impulsively or simplistically. In her innocence and primal wonder, all outcomes are new. She acts with thought but accepts the unexpected. The Superior Woman gains progress in her time to grow.

26. TA CH'U / THE WISEWOMAN (GROUNDING)

Above: Kên – Keeping Still, Mountain

Below: Ch'ien – The Labyris, Air

This hexagram belongs to the Wisewoman of matriarchy, the healer-teacher-sage. She represents the third aspect of the triple Goddess, Demeter, Hecate, Hel or Cerridwen, and the Crone or Hermit card in the Tarot. The hexagram pictures the labyris thought-strength of the universe within the grounding of a mountain, a reversal and a cosmic contradiction. Her three aspects are of holding strength – in restraint, unity and caring love.

The Wisewoman's hands deliver Daughters and ease pain. Her skill with herbs of healing, wise counsel, and gentle caring make her a mainstay of matriarchy. She has knowledge of the past, and applies her learning to the now. She is a grandmother aspect of the Goddess, crochet hook flashing beauty, stitching warmth, but can be of any age. In her Crone aspect, she represents too, the approaching darkness of death, and sees her not with terror but as rest, wisdom, rebirth, and the ultimate Mystery. If the Wisewoman withdraws from government in the community, choosing inner learning over action, she leaves the matriarchy to Daughters she has borne and trained. If she chooses to be active in government, she earns respect and recognition. However she makes use of her knowledge and wisdom, she benefits all.

THE CENTER – The Wisewoman. She is Strong and Grounded.

> The Wisewoman
> Is grounded
> And empowered.

The Wisewoman's strength and clarity is grounded in the universe and takes power from the earth. *Ch'ien* is the activity of creation, and *Kên* is unswerving integrity. By living connected to the earth and Wheel of Life, the Wisewoman continues in empowerment. Energy gathered by the strength of her self within and called upon in time. The Wisewoman is in balance with her universe, and her grounding offers good to all.

REFLECTION

> A labyris under the mountain:
> Grounding.
> The Wisewoman grows strong.

A labyris under the earth indicates great hidden power; in the wisdoms of matriarchy, women seek ways of understanding this life force of energy. The seeker learns not only from herstory, but from her Sisters, Mothers, the earth and her self-within. She grows into the skills of the Wise.

MOVEMENT

> *Nine at the beginning:*
> A challenge.
> She is grounded.

The woman seeks action, but her matriarchy bids her wait. She chooses grounding and restraint, and is correct. The Wisewoman finds good ways to show her caring. All things come in their time.

> *Nine in the second place:*
> Conflict.
> She waits.

Obstacles are overwhelming. The woman is blocked by conflicts on all sides and cannot act. She submits by holding firm and waiting for her time. Her knowledge is ready for the moment when she is needed. She triumphs in the end.

> *Nine in the third line:*
> The unity of
> Awareness.

Awareness opens a path. The woman follows and makes progress towards balance and unity. She is wary of the dangers of discord and conflict as she goes. The Wisewoman proceeds where she needs to go and learns self-protection as she goes there. She remains true to her values and gains peace.

>   *Six in the fourth position:*
>   Harmony and balance.
>   She is strong.

Unity and harmony in herself and in matriarchy create empowerment and strength. Her energy used for the good of all, she directs her actions well. The Wisewoman grounds herself in the universe, and achieves fulfillment and respect.

>   *Six in the fifth place:*
>   She cares
>   For her Sisters.

The Wisewoman helps her Sisters with her skills and uses her energy for good. She offers her knowledge to any who ask, and heals with their permission. Her roots are grounded in her Mother the earth. She uses her powers but does not take on more than she can handle. The blessings she sends return.

>   *Nine at the top:*
>   She gains the universe
>   By loving.

Conflicts end and wisdom is released; her Sisters recognize her skills and call on them in need. The Wisewoman grounded in caring, love and balance shapes her world.

27. I / PROVIDING NOURISHMENT (CARING)

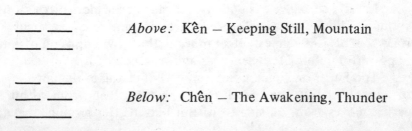

Above: Kên – Keeping Still, Mountain

Below: Chên – The Awakening, Thunder

The figure sketches an opening, and stands for nourishment of the body, mind and spirit. The three lower lines are physical fulfillment, while the upper trigram is the giving of spiritual caring.

A woman nurses her small Daughter at the breast. She provides her with nourishment that enables the child to live. As the Mother holds her infant she provides more than food. She offers warmth, safety, protection and love. Her caring fills needs beyond the physical, and her Daughter grows strong in mind and spirit as well.

THE CENTER — Temperate Fulfillment. Blessings.

> How she cares and
> What she cares for:
> Who she is.

In matriarchy, Sisters take care and are taken care of, and each receives what she needs. Women are part of the Goddess who nourishes all life. The Superior Woman cares for her less skilled Sisters, the strong woman helps the less strong, and all women in matriarchy are cared for this way. A strong woman is not sacrificed for the weak, nor a weak woman for the strong, yet Sisters are cared for by encouraging their skills and positive strengths. A woman who works to nourish the higher parts of her being is a Superior Woman, but greater or lesser strength, as well as mind, body and spirit have their place on the Wheel of Life.

REFLECTION

> Awakening the stillness:
> Providing nourishment.
> The Superior Woman is
> Temperate and caring.

In early spring, life is poised and ready at the moment of arousing stillness. The Goddess awakens on earth at Candlemas or Brigid, February 2. This is the time of quiet motion, the providing of nourishment in powerful potential for renewals about to burst forth.

The Superior Woman sees a model of caring in the nourishment of her spirituality: her speech moves out to others from within her; eating moves from outside to within herself. Her groundedness and temperance affect all. Temperate words are always proper and do not hurt other women, and temperate eating fulfills without upsetting herself. In caring, the Superior Woman gives and receives in quiet assurance. Power checked in temperance is the greater force.

MOVEMENT

> *Nine at the beginning:*
> She looks without
> Nourishment or caring.
> She errs.

The Superior Woman sustains herself spiritually from within. If she loses temperance, however, she no longer lives contented, but watches her Sisters with greed. Her envy arouses discord and she errs.

> *Six in the second position:*
> She receives
> Nourishment from others.
> She finds caring.

A Superior Woman makes her own living, but if she cannot, her Sisters or lover help her. If she does not provide for herself by choice, however, she is degraded at their support. In choosing to lose her self-reliance, the Sister loses her self-respect and finds caring bitter to take.

> *Six in the third line:*
> Rejecting real
> Sustenance.
> She is wrong.

An intemperate woman is never satisfied with what she has; pleasure alone gains no ends. The Sister is sated and still seeking; she is full but not nourished. No peace results from this road.

> *Six in the fourth place:*
> She seeks nourishment
> For her matriarchy.
> No error.

The line refers to a temperate woman of inner development and influence. Her skills offer caring to her Sisters, but she does not succeed alone. Her eagerness for help and knowledge radiates through the matriarchy. By working for the good of all, and beyond her own single nourishment, the Superior Woman goes on a quest for peace.

> *Six in the fifth place:*
>   She seeks help
>   From a Mother.
>   Nourishment.

A Superior Woman who wishes to provide nourishment in matriarchy feels that she lacks. She asks the help of a Mother who is competent and skilled but has kept to the background. Remembering humility, and not forgetting that her strength is aided, she succeeds for the good of all. To attempt achievement beyond her skills without the help of a guide brings error.

> *Nine at the top:*
>   The Goddess
>   Nourishes all.
>   Bright blessings.

The Superior Woman is aware of the Goddess as essence. In her inner knowledge, she gains fulfillment of even difficult tasks. Her actions and caring benefit her Sisters, her Daughters, her lover, the matriarchy and herself.

28. TAO KUO / INTERESTING TIMES

Above: Tui — The Joyous Daughter, Lake

Below: Sun — The Gentle Wind/Wood

The title *Interesting Times* replaces the original Chinese name of *Preponderance of the Great*. The renaming comes from the Chinese wry curse: May you live in interesting times. The hexagram is drawn of four unbroken yang lines within, and two shortened yin lines at the ends. The lines picture a weakened roof: she is solid in the middle, but without strength at the ends to hold her together. She is therefore doomed to break unless measures are taken to support and reinforce her. A period of interesting times in matriarchy is symbolized by this insecure state.

Yin and yang, in their earliest connotations, do not refer to warring forces but to complementary polarities. They are light and dark, active and receptive, upward and downward, moving and stationary, winter and summer, etc. Times of tearing down are opposite dualities to times of building. Yin and yang have each their places in the Superior Women and on the Wheel. Their positive balancing for correctness and good are the message of this hexagram.

THE CENTER — She knows When to Stop. Wise Judgment.

> Interesting times:
> The Superior Woman
> Withdraws from force.

The matriarchy is out of balance and exists in a state of precarious flux. Correct actions are needed to save the situation, decisive decisions and deeds. Strength is held centered but unrestrained, and her force is against cosmic harmony. Imbalance and discord in matriarchy are resolved through her Sisters by peaceful awareness and caring. With openness and consensus, differences are bridged; accord, balance and stability are regained. These are serious but not hopeless times.

REFLECTION

> Water over wood:
> Interesting times.
> The Superior Woman
> Withdraws unvanquished.

Force overwhelms in interesting times, a flood force destructive and out of control. She is a crisis while she lasts, but does not last long. The trigram *Sun* is the Tree of Life standing strong under water, and the trigram *Tui* is joy. The Superior Woman remains undespairing, though she chooses to withdraw for awhile.

MOVEMENT

> *Six at the beginning:*
>   She acts discreetly.
>   Wisdom.

Actions in interesting times require great discretion, and good groundwork at the outset is best. The Superior Woman moves slowly, builds gently and securely, and suffers no blame for her care.

> *Nine in the second position:*
>   Unexpected situations,
>   Fortunate ends.

The line refers to wood beside water, and symbolizes a dead tree that sends new growth from her base. What is thought lost is very much alive. In interesting times, the Superior Woman remains connected and grounded. By doing so, she finds return.

> *Nine in the third line:*
>   Too much pressure.
>   She breaks.

This is the woman who in interesting times refuses to wait. By her insistence on force she breaks the weakened roof. The Superior Woman knows when to stop and when to act; by adding careful support instead of stress she furthers.

> *Nine in the fourth position:*
>   Reinforcement.
>   All benefit.

By process of consensus, the matriarchy reinforces her goals and the threat of breakage is mended. The Superior Woman uses her strongest support and wisdom for the good of all.

> *Nine in the fifth place:*
>   An old tree blooms.
>   No rebirth.

The blooming of a tree out of season drains her resources. She does not fruit, and the flowers overextend her strength. There is no rebirth or gain here, and effects soon end. Only in outward appearance is there progress.

In interesting times, the Superior Woman seeks connection with her roots and triumphs. If she does not regain inner certainty, her renewal is an outward appearance that fails.

> *Six at the top:*
> She swims
> Beyond her depth.
> Danger.

Interesting times reach crisis and action here. The Superior Woman tries to save the situation by courage and valor, and she faces great danger in doing so. Heroic measures can fail or succeed. In an action that attempts to regain accord for matriarchy, there is risk but no wrong doing. As the Chinese ending of this hexagram states: "There are things that are more important than life."*

29. K'AN / THE DEPTHS

Above: K'an — The Chalice, Water

Below: K'an — The Chalice, Water

This is one of the eight hexagrams in *The Kwan Yin Book of Changes* composed of the same trigram above as below. *K'an* is the chalice, the depths, an immersion into dark, the intuitive mind. Cups are a suit in the Tarot, and *K'an* is The High Priestess in the Tarot's major arcana. When you draw the High Priestess card or *K'an*, "A wisdom is activated in you that is older and deeper than your ordinary emotions."† She is the essence of woman in matriarchy, the Priestess and Spiritual Woman.

K'an represents all-nurturing water. Water comes from the uni-

---

*Richard Wilhelm and Cary F. Baynes, Trans., *The I Ching or Book of Changes*, Bollingen Series XIX, (Princeton, NJ, Princeton University Press, 1950 and 1967), p. 114.
†Vicki Noble, *Motherpeace: A Way to the Goddess Through Myth, Art and Tarot*, (San Francisco, Harper and Row Publishers, 1983), p. 39.

verse, from the Goddess, and flows on earth in rivulets, channels and streams. She blends to form oceans, and water is the womb of the world. In women, the depths are feelings before thoughts, the intuitive before the apparent; the chalice is light within the darkness. In traditional *I Ching* commentaries, the hexagram emphasizes an aspect of danger, and *The Depths* is titled *The Abysmal*. In *The Kwan Yin Book of Changes* and the matriarchy, intuitive darkness is the brightest principle of all.

THE CENTER — Intuition and Feeling. She Flows Brightly.

> The Depths, water:
> By inward flow
> Bright blessings.

Water models correctness of action: she flows, fulfills and she nourishes. The Mother of Life, she remains unchanging in her own changing forms. Like her, the Priestess of matriarchy is open and true facing obstacles. By purity of spirit and by intuition she flows with her situations, and with inward understanding her actions resolve to the good. Her immersion into the depths brings births and blessings; water is the source of life.

REFLECTION

> Elemental water:
> The depths.
> The Priestess
> Flows brightly.

Water achieves by her flowing. She reaches into openings and depths, and fills them as she goes. She understands and penetrates the earth. The Priestess does the same: she immerses herself in inner knowledge, in intuition and connection with the Goddess. She travels darkly with the flow.

MOVEMENT

> *Six at the beginning:*
> She falls into
> Darkness flowing.
> New births.

In first entering the depths of intuition, the realms of water and darkness, even the Priestess loses her balance. She is unused to touching feeling and thinks she drowns. The Priestess gains her balance and she learns to swim. She does not drown being born.

Nine in the second place:
Water overwhelms.
She reaches slowly
And flows well.

Immersed in depths, the Priestess does not act without thinking, and she does not panic. She learns to feel and to use her senses; her skills begin to grow. From growth in slow and tentative beginnings, she flows to greater ends.

Six in the third line:
Water before
And water behind.
No turning back.

The Priestess is surrounded by her inner intuition, and she does not move forward or backward. She has not the experience to know where to turn or how to proceed. Realizing her position, she waits for advice and does not yet act.

Six in the fourth position:
The integrity
Of pure water.
She prospers.

Formalities are lessened in times of change, and inner qualities matter here, not their forms. Enlightenment comes in her kind, ornamentation only obscures her. Simple process leads to effectiveness in matriarchy.

Nine in the fifth line:
The depths
Fulfill.
Achievement.

Over-reaching is perilous in inner depths. The Priestess follows the least hindered paths to meet her needs. Her spirituality sustains her actions; she proceeds in peace and balance, and goes with the flow. She raises herself from her difficulties and achieves.

Six at the top:
>   She loses her
>   Intuition.
>   Drowning.

A woman hard-pressed by the depths of uncertainty loses her flow. She drowns in self-pity and self-doubt. The Priestess never loses her connection to the Goddess. She respects her mind and feelings as part of the cosmic all. By connection to her universe, by inner understanding, the Priestess proceeds calmly. She floats and does not fail.

30. LI / THE CARESSING FIRE

___ ___   *Above:* Li − The Wand, Fire
_____

_____   *Below:* Li − The Wand, Fire
___ ___

Li is the fire that shines, transforms and warms. She comforts the body and illuminates the mind. The repeated hexagrams show two long lines lit by the shortened line between them: the labyris universe merged with the pentacle earth. Fire caresses what she lights and burns; she has no shape of her own. She is the magick wand, the Great Goddess in her aspect of brightness, and shines upon love at her heights.

Fire is the southern direction, the time of noon and the sixth Chinese month of July and August. She is Leo in the zodiac, and rules the life force of energy and spirit. Fire heals, destroys and purifies in one. The wand represents all flamings, from candle to cookfire to the sun, and Wands are a suit in the Tarot. Fire's names are Brigid, Pele, Hesta and Vestia, all Goddesses of flame, volcano and hearth. Her colors are warm orange and golds, and the bright white of midsummer sunshine. She is fire opal and the lioness of the veldt, the dragon breathing flame under mountains, the spark-striking mares that pull daylight through the skies.*

---

*Starhawk, *The Spiral Dance: A Rebirth of the Ancient Religion of the Great Goddess*, (San Francisco, Harper and Row Publishers, 1979), p. 202.

THE CENTER — Caressing Touch. She Glows.

> The caressing fire:
> Light and brightness.
> They merge.

Light has darkness within her or she cannot prevail: dark is the complement to the bright. With yin and yang, the opposites and twins, one exists only with the other.

The sun caresses the moon and they illuminate and caress the earth. The Spiritual Woman is brightened by goodness, by the light of the Goddess that surrounds her, and she brightens matriarchy with her own inner light. Woman's life is part of the shining passion of the universe, and she warms in glowing peace. The Spiritual Woman lights her lover with brightness, and her lover lights the darkness that she finds. The bright and dark of both caress and touch and merge. In awareness, radiance and love, the Spiritual Woman finds her place.

REFLECTION

> Wand of light:
> The caressing fire.
> The Spiritual Woman
> Brightens matriarchy.

Both trigrams are light, and their repetition is the continuing of the life force. Brightness grows and wanes — in the day, in the moon, and in the year. Time repeats in her eternity of light and dark, of yin and yang. The Spiritual Woman reflects the circle dance of the universe. By her inner enlightenment, she illuminates her world.

MOVEMENT

> *Nine at the beginning:*
> Beginning dawn.
> Good intentions
> Are good days.

At dawn she wakes from sleep, as the Goddess wakes from sleep each year at Brigid. Her consciousness returns from the side of darkness, from intuitive waters to the life of energy and action. Light and dark connect and overlap. The Spiritual Woman is aware of dualities, and in her early waking she retains the psychic night. If she is open in her good instinct, she finds the light to see herself in both realms. Her clarity is the morning star, the light of all that comes.

> *Six in the second line:*
> Noon sun.
> Yellow sun.
> Warm actions.

Noontime, warmth, the Mother, summer: yellow is the color of earth, the color of warmth and middle acting, of the center. Yellow light in Chinese culture means blooming at her fullest. She is the balance of the middle way, and is the woman who lives on the spiral.

> *Nine in the third place:*
> Sundown.
> The Spiritual Woman
> Reaches wisdom.

Sunset is the ending day, and the ending of a year of life. All ends to rebegin and dies to be reborn. The Spiritual Woman accepts the cycle of the universe as unending freedom. She does not participate in intemperance or self-pity in her approaching age. Instead, she grows and validates her inner enlightenment by giving of what she learns.

> *Nine in the fourth position:*
> Falling stars.
> She does not
> Light and fade.

"Clarity of mind is rooted in life but can also consume . . . Everything depends upon how the clarity functions."* The Spiritual Woman is not a falling star that streaks across the sky and quickly fades. Instead, she burns with fuel in her fires, merging her light with darkness and is sustained. In acceptance of duality, of the Wheel of Life, light endures and prevails.

> *Six in the fifth place:*
> Water and fire,
> A slowing.
> Illumination.

---

*Richard Wilhelm and Cary F. Baynes, Trans., *The I Ching or Book of Changes*, Bollingen Series XIX, (Princeton, NJ, Princeton University Press, 1950 and 1967), p. 121.

At the peak of heat, awareness or love, the Spiritual Woman learns retreat to renew. If she proceeds, she burns out like the falling star of the fourth line. If she draws back, collects her energy and saves or even dampens her, she regains and recoups her power. The Spiritual Woman adds darkness to sustain her light, and does so at the moment to renew both. By this she gains clarity and illumination in her inner life.

> *Nine at the top:*
>> She shines for all,
>> She burns in all.*
>> Bright blessings.

The circle of the universe is in all. By accepting and identifying with the Wheel, by living within her wisely, the Spiritual Woman finds place in her universe and peace in her life. Her enlightenment brightens the matriarchy; she shines in all she does. When she loves, she loves completely and clearly. She walks in warmth and beauty wherever she goes, and her existence is a light to herself and the Sisters around her.

---

*Principle wiccan saying, in Starhawk, *The Spiral Dance: A Rebirth of the Ancient Religion of the Great Goddess*, (San Francisco, Harper and Row Publishers, 1979), p. 174.

The Hexagrams
Part II

© Robin Wood 1987

31. HSIEN / INFLUENCE (COURTSHIP)

Above: Tui — The Joyous Daughter, Lake

Below: Kên — Keeping Still, Mountain

The hexagram is composed of *Tui*, the joyous Daughter, and *Kên*, keeping still. The solid strength of a mountain influences the joy of a lake, and is the attraction of love between two Superior Women, love that is mutual, flowing and strong.

Where Part I of *The Kwan Yin Book of Changes* places emphasis on issues of the universe, spirituality, connectedness and inner growth, Part II emphasizes these values within the framework of living on earth. *Hsien*, the hexagram that opens Part II, considers the primary relationship, that of two women who are lovers and life partners. In addition, this hexagram involves a woman's influence on her world, her individual effect on matriarchy, and compares this relationship by the metaphor of courting a lover.

THE CENTER — Nothing Separates True Lovers. Peace.

> Courtship.
> Flowing love.
> Flowing peace.

The lake is above and the mountain below, strength and fluid joy. Opposites attract and meet to become one. Water remains water and earth remains earth, but together they are also something new. The lake nourishes the mountain, and earth upholds water. In their union, peace and love abound.

This is a relationship of balance and temperance. Joy flows in natural abundance and strength learns to yield. The goal is not merely seduction, but a courtship existing for pleasure and much more. Attainment here is the caring of shared love in women's lives. By the merging of two women who love each other, life on earth is affirmed. Through the influence of dual attraction, the Superior Woman influences her matriarchy; there is peace and harmony within the cosmic Wheel.

REFLECTION

> Joy on the mountain:
> Influence and courtship.
> The Superior Woman
> Gives and receives.

The mountain is nourished by a lake above her; she receives and benefits from the waters of joy. The Superior Woman likewise receives and gives. She gives of her love and accepts love, and in acceptance and giving two Sisters meet. In matriarchy too, the Superior Woman gives and receives in her influence.

MOVEMENT

> *Six at the beginning:*
> Intention to influence.
> No wrong.

Action begins with a thought-form, and thought is stronger than action. The intention to influence, to court a lover, is present here but no action is yet taken. In the intent is the manifest result. The Superior Woman who approaches her Sister in good faith receives no blame.

> *Six in the second place:*
> She waits to court.
> She prospers.

Actions rise from good intentions. Before she acts, the Superior Woman is aware of correctness. In proper time and with correct intent, she begins. The Superior Woman is sensitive to her Sister, and knows when to wait and proceed. Listening to her heart, she prospers gladly.

> *Nine in the third position:*
> She courts slowly.
> She cares.

Her heart leads her to action, and where hearts command the mind and body follow. Action without forethought, however, leads to error and rebuff. The Superior Woman does not court everyone she sees, nor gets involved with every Sister who seeks her out. She listens to her inner self. She does not take for granted a chance of real love, nor neglect to act on real caring. When she knows her heart, she knows when to hesitate and when to proceed. The Superior Woman moves forward with love, respect and caution. When she does so, she finds fulfillment and a union of joy.

> *Nine in the fourth place:*
> She courts with joy.
> Her heart is open.

The major line of this hexagram means that her heart is open to love. If her influence is enduring and correct, the Superior Woman is vulnerable without being hurt. She does not regret reaching out, but all who come under her influence are touched by her openness. She expresses her love and receives love in return, and two Sisters find each other at last. Action results in new beginnings, continuing brings joyous flow. There is mutual love between two strong and independent women.

> *Nine in the fifth line:*
> She is influenced
> And influences.

The Superior Woman is strong of will and determined in her love. She accepts her intuitive feelings, and without trying to change them, she lives and acts within their power. She influences her lover and is influenced in turn. They become a new force together, and they grow in their depths.

> *Six at the top:*
> Influence by mouth.
> No error.

The Superior Woman does not take part in idle influence, and her talk is not empty flirtation. Her actions speak louder than her words, and her actions and words are made from inner honesty. By transcending the superficial, she achieves the source, a love that flows from within.

32. HÊNG / DURATION (LOVERS)

Above: Chên – The Awakening, Thunder

Below: Sun – The Gentle Wind/Wood

Active *Chên* merges with the receptive *Sun*, the thunder with the gentle wind. These dualities are aspects in any relationship, two parts in every woman; they are bright and dark, yin and yang. Hexagram 31, *Hsien* is the hopeful courtship of two Sisters becoming lovers. *Hêng* is their partnership, their lifelong unity, respect and caring.

Two women exchange rings, the circle symbol of duration, to proclaim their union. With their Sisters in matriarchy they celebrate a ritual. Like the unending circle of the Wheel of Life, the women ask the Goddess for unending love, for caring that lasts their lifetimes.

THE CENTER – Enduring love. Unending Light.

> Enduring love
> Between women.
> The circle shines.

Endurance is progress toward a goal. She is not fixed but fluid, or wearing but she wears. She is the symbol of the circle, never ending without rebeginning, the promise of Goddess for the wholeness of all life. Enduring love is the subject of poetry, of women's art. She is the certainty of breathing, of the seasons, of the loved one's touch. Love between two Sisters is the constancy of the planets in their orbits, or constellations wheeling in their beauty through the skies. She is life giving, affirming and renewing, the meaning of the universe and earth.

The Spiritual Woman is dedicated to the ways of love. She endures in her relationships and in her life. She greets her lover with respect and cherishing. They care for and love each other, teach and learn together, but remain themselves. Two strong and independent

women in love are two who become one. In the meaning of their
enduring is the meaning of the Wheel.

REFLECTION

> Thunder awakens
> To the gentle wind:
> The Spiritual Woman
> Finds true love.

Thunder and wind are moving principles; thunder wakes the
storm, and wind refreshes the earth. Their movements and patterns
are the circle of the universe. They are the cycles of expansion and
contraction, cause and effect, beginning and process, elements that
wax and wane but always endure. The Spiritual Woman, awakened
and caressed, awakening and caressing in turn, endures and moves
and cycles in her love. She is flowing in her nature, and her love is
the purpose of her being.

MOVEMENT

Six at the beginning:
    Forced endurance.
    No success.
True love between Sisters comes by slow process of work and
understanding. The Spiritual Woman does not ask for duration too
soon. In the words of Lao-tse, "If we wish to compress something,
we must first let it expand."* Duration occurs in good time, and to
force her is to fail. The Spiritual Woman knows when to act and to
wait.

Nine in the second position:
    She speaks her heart
    And is not refused.
The Spiritual Woman opens herself to her lover. Although fearful of not being heard, or that she reaches too high, she speaks her
needs and feelings. She achieves duration and she knows her inner
heart. The Spiritual Woman is received with open arms.

---

*Quoted in: Richard Wilhelm and Cary F. Baynes, Trans., *The I Ching or Book of Changes*,
Bollingen Series XIX, (Princeton, NJ, Princeton University Press, 1950 and 1967), p. 127.

Nine in the third line:
> She has duration.
> She is strong.

A woman who listens to her Sisters but not to her inner self loses the constancy of her character. The Spiritual Woman is not swayed by stress, uncertainty or doubt. Her Sisters advise her, but only she knows her path.

Nine in the fourth place:
> She seeks
> In positive ways.

The Spiritual Woman does not seek duration where none exists, or searches forever and remains alone. She seeks in honesty and openness among Sisters of like mind, and there she finds enduring love.

Six in the fifth line:
> Continuing duration.
> Unending light.

Two Sisters who are lovers are independent individuals. Neither submerges her needs or ideas to the other, and neither is lost in the other or in their love. When women who love each other remain strong and whole, their merging is a thing of power and constancy. They are true to themselves and to each other, and build a love and life that grows and endures. Each brings her self to the relationship, and their duration brings them happiness and accord.

Six at the top:
> Enduring restlessness.
> She errs.

Continuing restlessness in a relationship overwhelms. True love partakes of certainty, peace and trust. Without these qualities of stability, she does not endure.

33. TUN / WITHDRAWAL

Above: Ch'ien — The Labyris, Air

Below: Kên — Keeping Still, Mountain

Tun is the sixth Chinese month of July and August, the wiccan Lammas and the zodiac sign of Leo. Summer has passed her zenith and winter appears on the horizon. "The Mother becomes the Reaper, the Implacable One who feeds on life that new life may grow."* The energy of beginnings is locked in grain that is not yet ready for harvest. The grain is potential; in her ripening she holds the rebirth of spring.

In the gain of cold and winter, endings begin; light withdraws and dark descends. Withdrawal is a law of the universe, a part of the natural Wheel. Beside darkness there is light; beside light there is dark. Both are fact, and neither exists without the other. There are times to continue and times to retreat and withdraw; neither is wrong in her place. Renewal is implicit in each ending and everything ends to rebegin.

THE CENTER — A Waning Time. Retreat in Joy.

> A time of
> Withdrawal.
> Grow darkly.

This is a time in which continuing does not succeed and progress is made indirectly. In periods of withdrawal, the Superior Woman recognizes her situation. She pulls back and learns to wait. Her withdrawal is not running away, a giving up or scattering of forces. Prudent withdrawal is wisdom and courage, a control and perception of her

---

*Starhawk, *The Spiral Dance: A Rebirth of the Ancient Religion of the Great Goddess*, (San Francisco, Harper and Row Publishers, 1979), p. 179.

needs.

In a political sense, retreat is a way toward action. By resisting wrongs quietly but withdrawing her skills from where they are misused, the Superior Woman acts by nonaction, by peaceful resistance, to catalyze change in her world. Creative withdrawal is a positive action; in knowing when not to use her skills, the Superior Woman applies them for good. By awareness and continuing, by connection with time and the spiral, the Superior Woman withdraws to proceed.

REFLECTION

> A mountain below the universe:
> Withdrawal or retreat.
> The Superior Woman
> Refuses wrong.

A mountain lifts towards sky but does not reach her: the air arcs upward, thought-form of the earth. The Superior Woman, like the labyris universe, knows when to withdraw. She shows the mountain's strength when she stops herself from reaching wrongly. Her integrity is as unconquerable as the air.

MOVEMENT

> *Six at the beginning:*
> Withdrawal in danger.
> She does not risk.

The Superior Woman follows her Sisters in withdrawal, and the danger is near. She attempts no action in a moment of peril and crisis. She risks nothing more, since now is not the time.

> *Six in the second line:*
> The lesser skilled
> Women withdraw.

In times of danger, women of matriarchy look to the Mothers for guidance. They follow her because they trust her judgment. The Superior Woman acts correctly in a time of adversity and makes her decisions with care. Her destiny is in balance, along with the well-being of her Sisters.

Nine in the third position:
> The Mothers take charge
> In withdrawal.

When withdrawal is necessary, Sisters look to the Mothers for leadership. This is not a time for consensus, as consensus has failed and the Sisters have taken no initiative. However reluctantly, the Mothers lead. The Superior Woman accepts the need for leadership, but returns her power to her Sisters as soon as possible. This is not a permanent way to govern matriarchy, but a temporary crisis.

Nine in the fourth place:
> She chooses withdrawal
> And change.

The Superior Woman knows when action only worsens her situation, and withdraws quietly, aware of her options. She takes the way of the most good, without compromising her integrity. By refusing her support and skills, the pressure of her resistance is a force for change.

Nine in the fifth line:
> Correct withdrawal.
> She is affirmed.

The Superior Woman sees her need and time to withdraw. She proceeds correctly, causes no conflict, and remains strong. Knowing what is correct, she does not change her mind; her continuing is affirmed.

Nine at the top:
> Patient withdrawal.
> She prevails.

Clarity is achieved and the Superior Woman has no doubts. She is reserved and patient, and does not choose in anger. With enlightenment and inner decision, the Superior Woman proceeds. She withdraws correctly and carefully but does so with certainty. Her awareness shows her when to return and brings her positive results.

34. TA CHUANG / JUSTICE (POWER)

Above: Chên — The Awakening, Thunder

Below: Ch'ien — The Labyris, Air

The trigrams are creative strength and awakening growth, and mean the merging of justice and power in the matriarchy and her women. The Chinese title of this hexagram is *The Power of the Great*, and represents the second Chinese month of March and April. In the Wheel of the Year, March and April are awakening months, times of rebirth and power. The Hopi call March Isumuya, Whispering Noises of Breezes, and April Kwiyamuya, the Windbreaker.* They are the time for plowing the fields, and a period too busy for major ritual. March 20 to April 20 in astrology is the zodiac sign of Aries, the Ram. She symbolizes "fire building within the earth — the fire of volcanos and the fire of growth — all things that signal a fresh start".† In the wiccan calendar, power has risen at spring equinox or Easter, when altars of early flowers celebrate the return of warmth and spring. The Wheel of the Year proceeds in justice and power, and women live within her natural law.

THE CENTER — Justice. Continuing Strength.

>   Balance and power.
>   Justice.
>   Strength continues.

The long lines representing strength are dominant, cautioning that too much power or force involve danger to the Superior Woman. She draws on her inner strength without disregarding justice and natural law. The shortened lines are growth and movement, and reminders

---

*Frank Waters, *Book of the Hopi*, (New York, Ballantine Books, 1963), p. 235.
†Geraldine Thorsten, *God Herself: The Frminine Roots of Astrology*, (New York, Avon Books, 1980), p. 355.

that in times of power, the Superior Woman moves correctly. True greatness is a merging of the qualities of power and justice, and this balance is the flow of the Goddess' universe.

REFLECTION

> Thunder in the air:
> Justice and power.
> The Superior Woman
> Walks in harmony.

Energy, the thunder represented by the Chinese dragon, ascends from underground to the skies of spring. Her awakening symbolizes the beginning of life on earth, the rebirth and fertility of the newly awakened Goddess. Spring is a time of awareness, of power in accord with the Wheel of Life. The Superior Woman uses strength for justice in her harmony with cosmic law.

MOVEMENT

> *Nine at the beginning:*
> Early power.
> She is warned.

Power exerted too soon or too strongly for the situation brings error. This line is a warning to the wise.

> *Nine in the second place:*
> She handles power
> Correctly.

Her road is visible and the Superior Woman proceeds without excess or force of any kind. By losing sight of her goals, or acting too soon or incorrectly, the Superior Woman risks error. In knowing when and how to act, she is empowered and achieves.

> *Nine in the third position:*
> The Superior Woman
> Respects her power.

A lesser skilled Sister falls into pride and a power-over situation, and is entangled in difficulty. The Superior Woman learns to avoid this error; she uses power carefully and wisely. She merges strength with correctness and uses them well.

Nine in the fourth line:
        Obstacles recede.
        Power furthers.
The Superior Woman proceeds with certainty and calm, and her sureness and wisdom dissolve all difficulty. She has no cause for regret in her actions, and her actions bring her growth. By tempering power correctly, the Superior Woman gains greatness for herself and her matriarchy. The less force she is involved with, the greater her power and strength.

Six in the fifth position:
        Outward harshness.
        Inner power.
A woman known for her toughness is correct and honest in her thinking and deeds. She appears harsher than she is. So long as she acts correctly and without excess, she achieves power without error.

Six at the top:
        A no-power situation.
        She waits.
In a winless situation, where she cannot take action or withdraw, the Superior Woman waits. By doing so, she regains her power and strength and asserts herself. She achieves her justice and goals in the end.

35. CHIN / SUCCESS

Above: Li — The Wand, Fire

Below: K'un — The Pentacle, Earth

© Robin Wood 1987

The figure shows sunrise, fire above earth. She represents success, sure progress and the steady growth of inner awareness and enlightenment. The sunrise, east, is connected in Hopi cosmology with birth and life. In wicca, dawn is the radiance of the Goddess, the rebirth of energy that makes the grain. A powerful affirmation, *Chin* is brightness, warmth and unfolding prosperity.

A woman writes a poem. Line by line she creates image, form and plot; her wand of progress is the pentacle of earth. In grounding and light, her thought-form comes alive and enters reality. She shares her sunrise and success with her Sisters.

THE CENTER — Attaining Progress. Blessings.

> Successful attunement.
> The Spiritual Woman
> Gains respect.

The Spiritual Woman gains awareness and certainty in relationships with her lover, her Sisters and herself. She is attuned to the Wheel of Life, to the Goddess. Using her skills for the good of all, the Spiritual Woman is recognized for her contributions and worth. She is dignified and patient. In her caring and giving, she is respected for all that she is, and her growth in matriarchy is a model of progress and success.

REFLECTION

> Morning sunrise:
> The image of success.
> The Spiritual Woman
> Dawns brightly.

Dawn is a time of clarity and revelation. Night recedes and day begins, the Wheel of Life goes on. Sunrise brightens and cleanses with her warmth; her rays reach out to enter women's being. The Spiritual Woman proceeds towards correctness in seeking success and the light.

MOVEMENT

> *Six at the beginning:*
> Success hindered.
> She goes on.

The Spiritual Woman needs signs of progress in her life; she is not always certain of her paths. She follows the ways of sunrise and peace, and does what she knows is correct. If she finds herself blocked, the Spiritual Woman remains grounded and waits. She does not force situations before their time. By her connection with the laws of universal order, with the Wheel of Life, the Spiritual Woman gains success.

Six in the second place:
> Progress in courtship.
> Their loving dawns.

Progress in courtship is uneasy and the Spiritual Woman does not succeed with her lover. She continues steadily in correct action. Her chosen lover notices her in time, and they find each other warmly. In her real caring and attraction, the Spiritual Woman perseveres.

Six in the third line:
> Correct clarity.
> No regrets.

The Spiritual Woman proceeds with actions that she knows are good. She receives no encouragement or blame from her Sisters in matriarchy. By her clarity, initiative and a knowledge of what is correct, she gains recognition and success.

Nine in the fourth position:
> She shares blessings.
> Bright sunrise.

A time of success is a time of clarity, when the hidden comes to light. The Spiritual Woman is generous with her skills and learning, and shares what she has. Her sunrise on this path is a bright one.

Six in the fifth line:
> Win or lose,
> She changes.

A principle of the Goddess universe is change. What feels at first like loss may be progress instead. The issue here is not that the Spiritual Woman wins or loses, but that her actions are correct. By choosing with inner clarity, she assures success to come.

Nine in the last place:
        Avoidance of force.
        She gains.

The Spiritual Woman knows that nothing is attained by force, and that force puts her goals in danger. By avoiding this, the Spiritual Woman avoids error, grief and inherent conflict. Force is contrary to natural law, and her avoidance brings power and peace.

36. MING I / ADVERSITY

Above: K'un — The Pentacle, Earth

Below: Li — The Wand, Fire

This hexagram is the opposite and complement to Hexagram 35, *Success.* The time of winter cold and waning light is symbolized by sunset, the sun's fire beneath the earth. In the last hexagram the Superior Woman met with unimpeded success in her endeavors; in *Adversity* she is hard-pressed. With grounding and inner awareness, the Superior Woman overcomes obstacles and changes adversity to success by her actions. A principle of the spiral is the necessity for change, and change is a law of the universe.

THE CENTER — Overcoming Adversity. She Endures.

        Sunset,
        Adversity and waning.
        She prevails.

The Superior Woman is not overwhelmed by her times. She controls her life and changes destiny by her actions. With calm strength and certainty, the Superior Woman learns to protect herself.

Although open to ideas and women around her, she chooses her way. By these means, she prevails against difficulties and creates her own success.

There are times of adversity when the Superior Woman obscures her skills for awhile. She conserves her energies and is ready to return when she may. Success is not lost by this choice. When her Sisters are able to open to her, the Superior Woman is waiting and supportive. By her endurance in situations of incorrectness around her, she shields and protects her light.

REFLECTION

> Sunset on earth:
> Adversity.
> The Superior Woman waits.

In adversity, the Superior Woman does not engage in conflict or attempt to force her ideas. She knows when to withdraw and wait for change. She allows her pain to pass into the earth, to the all-receiving Mother, and does not show her hurt to her Sisters. A time of adversity changes in the nature of all things. The Superior Woman succeeds in accord at last.

MOVEMENT

> *Nine at the beginning:*
> Adversity and retreat.
> Great sadness.

The Superior Woman meets a situation in which she cannot prevail; she has no peace and finds no comfort or support among her Sisters. In holding firm to her inner integrity she suffers alone. The Superior Woman sees clearly and does not lose sight of her path. Although she feels lost and isolated, she does not falter. Her adversity and distress are intense, but temporary.

> *Six in the second line:*
> She acts correctly
> And wins.

The Superior Woman is hurt in her correctness, but hope comes with her choices and actions. She accepts her pain, and works for her matriarchy and her Sisters. She resolves the conflict and prevents worse harm. Her selflessness for the greater good wins peace.

Nine in the third place:
> Confronting in haste.
> She does not change.

The Superior Woman meets a source of disharmony and adversity. She attempts confrontation but fails at change. All things occur in their time, and the time is not now. Forcing the issue does not bring resolution.

Six in the fourth position:
> Dialogue fails.
> She retreats.

The Superior Woman dialogues with her source of adversity but the time is not yet correct. Dialogue fails and peace is not achieved. The Superior Woman does not accept blame or engage in self-blame or pity. In a moment of darkness, she is strong and clear on her paths.

Six in the fifth place:
> She holds firm
> And wins.

In a time when integrity is not recognized or respected, the Superior Woman chooses to act. By not withdrawing from adversity, she faces struggle but not defeat. The Superior Woman grounds her courage and protects herself from hurt. By steady truth and inner clarity, she wins.

Six at the top:
> Adversity defeats adversity.
> The light returns.

At peak of full darkness, light returns; all ending are beginnings on the Wheel of Life. Adversity overwhelms the woman who opposes her, but adversity is defeated by her own nature. Adversity defeats adversity, and the Superior Woman overcomes. As the Wheel swings ever upward, there is change and a new dawn.

37. CHIA JÊN / THE MATRIARCHY

——— ———
——— ———   *Above:* Sun — The Gentle Wind/Wood
——— ———

——— ———
——— ———   *Below:* Li — The Wand, Fire
——— ———

   This hexagram is the matriarchy and the women who make their lives within her. The six lines symbolize the Priestess, the Mother, the Wisewoman, the Superior and Spiritual Woman, her lover/partner, and young Daughter. All aspects of the circle are examined here, but each of the six family functions exists in every woman. Leadership in matriarchy is the responsibility of every Sister. All learn and teach, and all grow in harmony and strength. The matriarchy operates as a whole, and benefits from the individual skills of all. Each woman is the matriarchy, and without her she could not exist.
   Harmony in the single couple, or single circle within matriarchy, reflects on peace within society as a whole. This unity mirrors the oneness of the earth, which in turn reflects the oneness of the universe. The Goddess operates in everyone and is a part of all. In the Tarot, this hexagram is The World.

THE CENTER — Matriarchy. She is Blessed.

> The Matriarchy.
> Family of Woman.
> Blessed be.

   The strength of matriarchy is the bond between lovers. This relationship is mirrored in the love of women for each other as Sisters and co-workers, and the love of women for the common good. The constancy and caring of lovers who are partners is a combination of action and thought in both. When these qualities are in balance, the relationship is stable and respectful, and is seen in all aspects of daily life.

The Mother teaches her Daughter and learns from the Priestess. The Wisewoman heals and counsels, and learns from the child. The Sisters learn, and give of their learning, and they share and teach. The skills of one complement the skills of another, and the matriarchy needs every skill. In the strength and caring of women is the strength and caring of the Goddess. The matriarchy blossoms and grows.

REFLECTION

> The wind birthed in fire:
> An image of matriarchy.
> Continuing peace.

Energy as heat is imaged by the wind-stirred flame, wind rising from the wand of fire. The spiral radiates from her core, from the individual Sister to her lover, to the matriarchy as a whole. To be effective in matriarchy, the Superior Woman begins with confidence in herself. Her confidence leads to respect and confidence in her lover. Their integrity and openness are part of their inner lives, and implicit in their actions. Their actions together reflect on their movements and effectiveness in the circle. Strength, steadiness, integrity, respect — these are qualities of women in the matriarchy.

MOVEMENT

> *Nine at the beginning:*
> The Priestess teaches.
> Bright blessings.

Each member of matriarchy has her role in the circle, but the roles overlap and are interchangeable among Sisters. While the Priestess has the governing skills of a Mother, she chooses to turn inward to the Mysteries instead. Her choice brings good fortune, and her skills benefit all.

> *Six at the second line:*
> The Mother governs
> By consensus.

The Mother is the center of matriarchal government. She is a leader who gathers women together by consensus. The Mother takes no choices against her Sisters' will; she does not rule, she facilitates.

She comforts and nourishes her Sisters, and walks in ways of unity among them. She creates peace from discord, order from confusion, by her skills with groups and her love.

> *Nine in the third place:*
> The Wisewoman heals
> And is respected.

The Wisewoman withdraws from the governing of matriarchy to develop her inner skills. Unlike the Priestess, she does not lead spiritually, but seeks solitude and chooses to learn alone. Although she does not participate in process, she is part of her society. When she chooses to return, she has much to teach, and she who is taught or healed by her is blessed.

> *Six in the fourth line:*
> The Superior Woman —
> She shines.

The circle is composed of Superior and Spiritual Women. Each Sister has a skill to offer, something to teach or to learn. Each gives and each receives. Every Sister contributes what she can and adds her love. In this way matriarchy is built and grows certain, and the women within her shine.

> *Nine in the fifth position:*
> Lovers are the light
> Of the world.

The mutual relationship of caring, respect and love between two Sisters is the root of matriarchy's strength. In love between two women is the model for unity in women's world. By their integrity and cooperation the matriarchy is made real and whole. Lovers contain the light of the universe within their arms.

> *Nine at the top:*
> The Daughter is
> Cherished and taught.

The Daughter is matriarchy's future. She is protected and helped to understanding, taught to think clearly, to act spiritually and well. Given freedom and independence with guidance, she is bright and gentle in her growing power and she knows no fear. Some part of her remains in us all.

38. K'UEI / OPPOSITION

```
━━━  ━━━        Above:  Li – The Wand, Fire
━━━━━━━


━━━  ━━━        Below:  Tui – The Joyous Daughter, Lake
━━━━━━━
```

Flames rise above, and water flows inward and away from her. The two elements are shown in opposition in this hexagram, and opposition is the theme of the reading.

A woman gives her Sister a polarity massage, and with the balancing of opposite energies comes healing. Although stressed and scattered at the beginning, both healer and the woman healed are grounded into harmony by the process. The balancing of energies ends an inward opposition, leaving the Sisters bonded and whole. Opposition in matriarchy is met by the balancing of polarities and is resolved.

THE CENTER – Opposition. Cautious Balancing.

> Opposition.
> Cautious balancing.
> Small motions favor.

In a period of conflict and discord in matriarchy, the women cannot handle major goals. Consensus is not reached and agreement is not made; feelings are too strong. Attempted force makes matters worse and widens the imbalance. The discussion opposed is tabled for awhile, and smaller tasks are taken care of first. Good outcomes are gained in lesser decisions, and by their progress paths are opened for greater things to come.

Opposition represents dualities, and the matriarchy remains strong if her time is slowly eased. In the turning of the cosmic Wheel there are always two sides to be balanced. Opposition has her place in matriarchy as well as in the universe. Polarities are resolved, and change to fertile creativity in the end.

REFLECTION

> Fire over the lake:
> Opposition.
> The Wheel of Change.

As primary elements, fire and water remain themselves. In their example, the Superior Woman retains her integrity in opposition. Within the laws of nature and change, she prevails at last.

MOVEMENT

> *Nine at the beginning:*
> Correct behavior.
> No error.

In a period of opposition, the Superior Woman proceeds with correctness. She sees the necessity for accord, but does not force decisions before their time. When Sisters are alienated, the situation is temporary and resolution follows. The Superior Woman proceeds with care and avoids conflict; she does not place pressures that lead to anger. By her correctness she continues without error.

> *Nine in the second position:*
> They cannot meet
> But do meet.

In the course of events, two women of matriarchy find pain in working together. An unexpected encounter between them melts the ice. They realize each other as Sisters, though their ideas oppose.

> *Six in the third line:*
> Two lovers oppose.
> Eventual peace.

Two lovers face conflict in everything they do, and everything opposes their relationship. Whatever her obstacles, however, the Superior Woman continues to love. She is not defeated by adversity and remains constant and understanding. With good attitude, the lovers work things out.

> *Nine in the fourth place:*
> Her loneliness opposes.
> She waits.

The Superior Woman finds herself alone, without lover or friend. She holds to her ideals, to what she truly believes in, and waits for the Wheel to turn. She meets another woman, and their polarities attract. They recognize each other and discover love. The Superior Woman opposes loneliness and mistrust; She finds a lover and is not alone.

Six in the fifth line:
> She achieves openness
> And balance.

The Superior Woman meets a Sister she does not at first accept. In time, the Sister's honesty and brilliance are apparent, and she is respected and welcomed. The Superior Woman's opposition gives way to balance and warmth.

Nine at the top:
> Opposition within.
> She changes and grows.

Opposition is inward. The woman misunderstands her Sisters and believes them insincere. She closes herself to consensus, becomes defensive and engages in conflict. With mediation and inner awareness, she realizes her error. The Superior Woman apologizes and changes the tensions and discord. She turns the Wheel and matriarchy grows.

39. CHIEN / OBSTRUCTION

Above: K'an — The Chalice, Water

Below: Kên — Keeping Still, Mountain

Water ahead and mountains behind: *Chien*, the hexagram for obstruction. The Superior Woman is on a precipice, from which she can step neither forward nor back. The mountain represents stillness, however, and by stillness and waiting the Superior Woman achieves. Obstructions are there to be surmounted, and the commentaries discuss how.

A rockslide obstructs the path of a woman's plow at planting time. She cannot move the boulders and earth alone, and seeks ways to overcome the obstacle. She engages the help of her Sisters and together they clear the debris. By making correct choices, the Superior Woman best cares for her life. She finds ways to remove the rockfall or to use her for good.

THE CENTER — Obstruction. She Endures to Gain.

> Obstruction.
> Withdraw to proceed.
> Achievement.

The Superior Woman's obstacles seem overwhelming. She does not act alone, but in reviewing her situation, she chooses to withdraw. She asks for help from her Sisters and receives their willing skills. The Mothers provide guidance, and the Superior Woman returns to her challenge and succeeds. Obstructions in this hexagram are temporary; they are there to remove and change.

REFLECTION

> Water and mountains:
> Obstruction.
> The Superior Woman
> Overcomes.

Learning to overcome obstructions makes a woman strong and independent. She faces greater challenges and she grows. The Superior Woman takes charge of her own actions and removes obstacles from within. She gains improvement by taking control of her life.

MOVEMENT

> *Six at the beginning:*
> She first holds back.
> No blame.

A woman facing obstruction does not jump in without fore-thought; she holds back long enough to assess her situation. With thorough understanding of her problem, the Superior Woman acts correctly and achieves.

Six in the second line:
    She faces conflict
    Not her own.
Some obstructions are met directly and head on. The Superior Woman does not wait to act when the matriarchy needs her, when her Sisters need her, or when there is no other way or better time. She is placed in the circumstance through no fault of her own, but by decisiveness and good choices she triumphs.

Nine in the third position:
    She values her worth.
    Greater good.
The Superior Woman acts in service of her Daughters and Moth-ers, but unnecessary risk does not help them. Self-sacrifice is brave and usually senseless, leaving those behind her in need. The Superior Woman accomplishes what she can; she learns prudence, and knows her own strength and worth.

Six in the fourth place:
    Aid from her Sisters.
    Continuing flow.
The obstruction is more than the Superior Woman can manage alone. She realizes this and asks help, and her Sisters in matriarchy are there for her. By waiting and acting together, the Superior Woman with her Sisters succeeds.

Nine in the fifth line:
    Serious difficulty.
    The women answer.
The Superior Woman comes to her Sister's aid; she does not avoid obstacles or hesitate in a crisis. By acting for others in selfless-ness, the Superior Woman is helped and guided to succeed. In the united strength of matriarchy, danger and obstructions are removed.

Six at the top:
>A wisewoman returns.
>No obstruction.

A Wisewoman is withdrawn from matriarchy for solitude and study; in a period of obstruction, she is tempted to remain away. The Wisewoman does not separate herself from her Sisters' danger, but recognizes the danger as her own. She returns to activity, and her learning helps matriarchy triumph. When crisis ends, the Wisewoman returns to her solitude, and the love and respect of her Sisters goes along.

40. HSIEH / RELEASE

_____ _____
_____ _____   *Above:* Chên — The Awakening, Thunder
_____

_____
_____ _____   *Below:* K'an — The Chalice, Water
_____ _____

Hsieh reflects release of the obstructions and oppositions of Hexagrams 38 and 39. After conflict there is resolution; after labor, rebirth. There is easing of tension and frustration. The Wheel turns in sequence with change and new beginnings; a time of peril ends with release.

A woman labors in childbirth. She presses against the will of the child being born. Her Sisters watch with her and aid her in the process through the night. With the crowning of a Daughter's head at dawn, release begins. Labor ends with the affirming of new life.

THE CENTER — Release of Tension. She Starts Change.

>Release.
>The turning
>Of the Wheel.
>She changes and flows.

The hexagram indicates a sudden lifting of stressful situations. The Superior Woman returns to her daily path refreshed, and is energized and released from great cares.

The Superior Woman avoids excess in her new release. She does not say "I told you so" or boast of her wins, but celebrates with her Sisters and returns to normal work. In doing this she earns respect. She ends obstructions quickly and without delay.

REFLECTION

> Thunder and rain:
> Release.
> The Superior Woman
> Is a rainbow.

Chên is thunder and *K'an* is water; a rainstrom clears the air. With the fading of thunder and the halt of rain, the earth is cleansed to begin a new cycle. The Superior Woman lets go of her past oppositions and releases her former obstructions. She proceeds on her Wheel and is renewed. From endings flow new beginnings; a rainbow appears in the sky.

MOVEMENT

> *Six at the beginning:*
> Healing and
> Recovery.
> Release.

A time of confrontation, blockage, labor or frustration is over. The Superior Woman is released from struggle and pain and finds peace. She takes the healing process into herself; she rests.

> *Nine in the second place:*
> Strength in
> Moderation.
> Good release.

The Superior Woman sets her actions and awareness on the problem of release. She attains her goal and grows strong from the process, and is part of the harmony of her world.

Six in the third position:
>She takes
>Without giving.
>Wrong release.

A woman in need is helped by her Sisters. She is given a time of healing, protection and ease. She takes her release for granted, however, and does not respond when her Sisters need her. The Superior Woman accepts times of receiving and is able to receive; she accepts times of giving, and learns to give. Her release is in balance in all things.

Nine in the fourth place:
>Released
>Independence.
>She is strong.

The Superior Woman finds a Sister too dependent upon her. She helps her as asked, but the greater good is in teaching her Sister independence. The Superior Woman lends strength and receives strength, and grows stronger in the exchange.

Six in the fifth line:
>She releases
>Uncertainty.
>She grows.

Rescue comes from within. The Superior Woman takes control of situations, and she finds release. Her certainty and inner strength lift opposition and bring her success. She directs her own life and her fate.

Six at the top:
>Releasing
>Obstruction.
>She is free.

By awareness and clarity, the Superior Woman lifts inner obstacles. She finds the answers within herself, and puts her release into action. The Superior Woman makes her own destiny and renewal. She frees herself, gives birth to new ideas, and prevails.

41. SUN / RESTRAINT (LESSENING)

Above: Kên — Keeping Still, Mountain

Below: Tui — The Joyous Daughter, Lake

Sun is a lake at the foot of a mountain, water below earth. The lake is joyous and innocent, flowing freely and broadly in every direction; the mountain is steady and solid and does not yield. Keeping still teaches and calms the lake, channels and directs her energies in careful restraining. In the lessening of flow, the lake gains purpose and grows stronger. This is also an example in matriarchy, where a Daughter is taught by the Mothers in firmness and gentleness. In the restraint and lessening of aimless energies, the Daughter learns purpose and control.

THE CENTER — Restraint and Lessening. She Grows.

> Restraint.
> The Spiritual Woman
> Lessens to gain.

Restraint and letting go are two phases of the Lady Moon, and both parktake in universal balance. Beginning and ending, waxing and waning, blooming and decay are all part of the Wheel of Life and good in their proper places: the message of this hexagram is in awareness of the times. A period of low fortune may bring about a growth in spirituality of inner perception. Plain honesty and connectedness are keys to turning less into more. Inner values are greater than external and material ones, and a show of outward gain is not needed. Even in moments of lessening and restraint, the Spiritual Woman carries a full heart.

REFLECTION

> The lake at mountain's foot:
> Restraint or lessening.
> The Spiritual Woman
> Channels her directions.

Water is flowing and boundless and the mountain is a moveless strength that curbs her. The mountain in excess is rocky and obstinate; the lake in excess is undirected rapids. Each benefits from decrease by the other. The mountain's strength is gentled by flow and made less rigid by the water's freedom and ease. The lake is channeled and taught by mountain stillness, and is held in check. By restraint and lessening of external energies, both mountain and lake grow in power.

MOVEMENT

> *Nine at the beginning:*
> Giving and restraining.
> The Sisters are considerate.

The Spiritual Woman, when her work ends, offers help to a Sister and they work together. The Sister is concerned for her helper: Is she tired? Is she strong enough to do two tasks? Is the Sister who is aided carrying her share? Spiritual Women are considerate of each other's energies, and less at this time may be more. The Sister knows what she needs and what she can do for herself. The Spiritual Woman is aware of how help affects her Sister's independence, of how much help is too much, and both are sensitive to the occasion.

> *Nine in the second place:*
> The Spiritual Woman
> Does not lessen herself.

Self-awareness, perception and restraint are qualities of the Spiritual Woman, and she is dignified in all things. She retains her integrity and does not trivialize her skills. The Spiritual Woman's service profits herself and her matriarchy because she does not lessen her own worth. She continues this path to success.

> *Six in the third line:*
> Three women travel.
> Two are lovers.

Three women travelling join their energies and companionship
for a journey. They work and play together along the way, and are
the root foundation of community. When one of them reaches her
destination, the number is lessened to two. The two remaining focus
on each other and each other's needs. They discover mutual affinities
and become lovers.

Six in the fourth position:
    A woman restrains error
    Her Sisters support her.
The Spiritual Woman learns to recognize and lessen her errors.
Her Sisters realize her efforts and are supportive of her development.
The Spiritual Woman, by her simplicity and clarity, eases her Sisters'
tensions concerning her as she eases her own. Channeled flow then
follows. By restraining her faults, all gain.

Six in the fifth place:
    A time of love
    Unlessened.
An effect of restraint is increase. In a time of controlled energies
and the prosperity of being loved, the Spiritual Woman meets un-
lessened bounty. Her Sisters smile at her, and nothing restrains her
joy.

Nine at the top:
    She gains without
    Lessening others.
A Priestess channels energy and blessings to the matriarchy, and
any woman may become a Priestess. She passes her skills on to others,
teaching her Sisters development and growth. The Spiritual Woman
benefits her matriarchy when she restrains to increase herself; none
are deprived or lessened by anything she gains. As she grows in
empowerment, the Spiritual Woman brings empowerment to her
community.

42. KUAI / RESOLUTION (PROGRESS)

Above: Tui — The Joyous Daughter, Lake

Below: Ch'ien — The Labyris, Air

Kuai shows progress through resolution, and her Chinese title is *Break-Through*. The lake progresses beyond the labyris universe to reach new heights of fulfillment. Growth is indicated in the Superior Woman and her matriarchy, a growth both outward and within. The month is April-May, the Chinese third month, which is Aries and Taurus in the zodiac; she is wands (spring) in the Tarot, and the time from spring equinox to Beltane in wicca. Resolution is the incoming tide of life's promise. In the period that culminates in Beltane's love and passion, the Goddess renews the earth. The fields grow green and new, the air is clean; the Maiden makes ready to become Mother. This is the waxing of the life force: obstacles dissolve, and a break-through in progress is at hand.

THE CENTER — Resolution and Progress. Union.

> She achieves both
> Passion and reason.
> She resolves.

Passion and reason coexist, and correctness controls and complements them. The Superior Woman chooses respect and awareness in her attitudes towards both. Resolution is a union of certainty and gentleness, in which the balance of passion and intellect is recognized and fulfilled. Desire flows in the Superior Woman as part of her natural spiral. In her oneness of body and spirit, she gains unity and resolve.

---

*Hexagrams 42 and 43 are reversed from the traditional use intentionally. By reversing them, the seasons fall in order, rather than April-May following May-June.

REFLECTION

> The lake above the universe:
> Resolution and progress.
> The Superior Woman
> Shares fulfillment.

The lake rises to meet the sky and is received. She fills with passion and desire, and all that fills then empties in the law of change. The Superior Woman flows with love and feeling. She shares these rituals, or loses their blessings as they change. "Power-from-within is the power of . . . the dark; the power that arises from our blood."* and passion in love is the Goddess' gift. In the progress of her inner development, the Superior Woman remains open to resolution and progress.

MOVEMENT

> *Nine at the beginning:*
> She dives in.
> No blame.

Beginnings of love or progress are tenuous and obstacles remain. The Superior Woman acts but not in haste. She evaluates her strength in the situation before making her move, and enters the waters with caution. Diving in without forethought and planning leads to error.

> *Nine in the second place:*
> Cautious resolution.
> She approaches.

Resolve and prudence complement and aid each other. The Superior Woman is ready but does not act without planning. She is prepared for alternate approaches and is not taken unaware. Tempered with respect and reason, her desires fulfill in good progress.

> *Nine in the third position:*
> She is resolved
> In feeling.

The Superior Woman holds to what she feels. Her Sister differs

---

*Starhawk, *Dreaming the Dark: Magic, Sex and Politics*, (Boston, Becaon Press, 1982), p. 4.

with her analysis, and she faces a time of loneliness and celibacy. The Superior Woman endures in her resolve and progress in her goals. Despite setbacks, she is recognized at last, and not alone.

> *Nine in the fourth line:*
> Uncertain progress.
> She finds pain.

The woman wishes to progress but the time is not ready for a break-through. She faces obstacles and conflict with her Sister and within herself. Her stubbornness causes her inner pain, but she does not let go or yield. Resoluteness in seeking progress is unfounded for now.

> *Nine in the fifth place:*
> She swims
> With the Wheel.

The Superior Woman swims in the center of the Wheel of Life; she remains connected and certain in her desires, but within the time at hand. In certainty she continues, and is welcomed at last.

> *Six at the top:*
> ·　Cautious resolution.
> She flows.

Passion is resolved and tensions released, with no detail overlooked or underestimated. The Superior Woman as she celebrates remains alert and cautious to what is not readily apparent or seems minor. She attains resolution and gains progress in her goals and her love.

43.　I / LETTING GO (GAINING)

Above:　Sun – The Gentle Wind/Wood

Below:　Chên – The Awakening, Thunder

The awakening Goddess is late spring, a union of the universe with the earth. She is the primal time of letting go, of sexual celebration, of gaining and release, the brief time of hope's bursting forth into fulfillment. "Everything speaks with passion: the fields, the mountains, the trees, the birds, the children. Everything shines from inside out, and everything has a dark, secret core where power lies."* The awakening thunder and gentle wind rouse to stir the life force. The time is Taurus and Gemini, the Chinese fourth month of May and June, the period from Beltane to the summer solstice. Spring in full bloom is short and happens all at once.

THE CENTER — Letting Go and Gaining. She Merges.

> Letting go and gaining.
> She merges
> With prosperity.

In times of *Restraint* (Hexagram 41), a holding back or decrease of energy results in positive gain. In *Letting Go*, her duality and outcome, success occurs by release of effort and persistence. The Superior Woman merges her energies to the matriarchy's work, and knows her opportunity is now. She gives of herself, lets go of her powers, her joys and her skills. The season of spring flowering is short, as is any time of fulfillment and letting go. The Superior Woman recognizes this, and makes good use of her prospects.

REFLECTION

> Spring breezes and thunder:
> Letting go.
> The Superior Woman
> Gains correctness.

The gentle wind and awakening thunder gain to let go of each other, and the Superior Woman gains and releases in self-awareness. When she chooses a Mother or Priestess for role model, the Superior Woman learns from her all she can. When she realizes an error in herself, she lets go of her faults and becomes free. When she chooses

---

*Starhawk, *Dreaming the Dark: Magic, Sex and Politics*, (Boston, Beacon Press, 1982), p. 93.

a lover, the Superior Woman does so in release and joy. Inner awareness used for betterment and growth is spirituality's highest gain.

MOVEMENT

> *Nine at the beginning:*
> She continues her work.
> She gains blessings.

The Superior Woman asks help from the Goddess and receives her from within. She uses her gains for achievements she would not have reached before. Letting go is implicit in service and giving. The Superior Woman who receives to share her blessings finds love and inner peace.

> *Six in the second line:*
> She gains in harmony
> By letting go.

The Superior Woman gains by releasing her potential for action, and is grounded in knowledge of the ways of the Wheel of Life. She achieves what she works for by acting in accord and cooperation; she remains strong, connected and stable in letting go. The Superior Woman's deeds and choices have impact on the universe and matriarchy; they work for her own and her Sisters' good.

> *Six in the third place:*
> Positive lives.
> She gains love.

A time of gain and letting go is so powerful that even the commonplace becomes extraordinary. The Superior Woman acts correctly out of connectedness and balance. She meets a Sister who becomes her lover in a time of release and joy. She shows her positive outlook to all she meets.

> *Six in the fourth position:*
> She walks a centered path.
> She gains.

A woman of matriarchy has skills to mediate between Sisters and bring matters of conflict to agreement. This gift is not withheld, but is an aspect of letting go and gain in matriarchy. The Superior Woman walks a centered path that leads to good release.

Nine in the fifth line:
>She gains.
>Blessed be.

The Superior Woman who is gentle is appreciated by her Sisters and rewarded and recognized in all she does. The matriarchy supports and welcomes her deeds, and gains from the blessings of her love and presence.

Nine at the top:
>She lets go
>And gains prosperity.

The Superior Woman gives and lets go of her skills and love for the good of all. She asks no price for her giving, and she gives from the heart. The more that she chooses to give, the more the Superior Woman has to give. The more that she gives, the more she receives. By letting go, the Superior Woman brings gain and release to herself and to many. Prosperity and love increase for her and her Sisters.

44. KOU / COMING TO MEET

Above: Ch'ien — The Labyris, Air

Below: Sun — The Gentle Wind/Wood

The hexagram describes the beginning darkness, the yet unnoticed shortening of light. In the trigrams, the winds of change rise gently to meet the universe, and are a coming together of seasons. Summer wanes gradually to fall, and fall darkens to become winter before the new spring.

Kou is June-July, the fifth month in the Chinese calendar, Kamuya and Kelemuya in the Hopi. Astrologically, she is Cancer, the summer solstice, and is celebrated as Midsummer's Night or Litha in

the circle. The longest day and shortest night of the year, brightness
has reached her peak and begins to wane. The Kachinas leave the
Pueblos at Niman Kachina for six months in other worlds, and approaching darkness comes to meet the fullest sun.

THE CENTER — Coming to Meet. Supreme Good.

> Coming to meet:
> Affinities complement.
> The women rejoice.

Polarities attract, and their meetings become universal in completeness. "The important part of the yin/yang symbol is not the
black part or the white part or the way they balance or contrast with
each other. The important part is the circle that unites them."* All
principles are parts of the whole, and they participate in the flow of
the universe.

Coming to meet has great significance, for the meeting is of the
seasons, the universe and the earth. When two women come to meet
in an act of love, there is prosperity and joy. In the Richard Wilhelm
and Cary F. Baynes traditional translation of the *I Ching*, The Judgment reads: "Coming to meet. The maiden is powerful".†

REFLECTION

> Below the universe, the gentle wind:
> The image of coming to meet.
> Completeness begins her motion.

The wind touches everything under the universe, and connects
the sky and the land; her effects extend to all. The effects of coming
to meet — on two women's lives, on matriarchy and in the circle of
the seasons — are profound. A gentle wind stirs the universe to action.
By coming to meet, earth and sky are made one.

---

*Gail Fairfield, *Choice Centered Tarot*, (Seattle, Choice Centered Astrology and Tarot, 1982), p. 30.
    †Richard Wilhelm and Cary F. Baynes, Trans., *The I Ching or Book of Changes*, Bollingen Series XIX, (Princeton University Press, 1950 and 1967), p. 171.

MOVEMENT

> *Six at the start:*
>> Cautious awareness.
>> She endures.

Women steer their destinies by chosen actions. With caution and awareness, the Superior Woman waits for the right time and does not come to meet in haste.

> *Nine in the second line:*
>> Quiet reserve.
>> Correctness.

The Superior Woman comes to meet gently and with dignity; her reserve furthers everything she does. By awareness of the spiral and the Wheel of Life, by her groundedness, she proceeds correctly in her attraction and has no regrets.

> *Nine in the third place:*
>> Uncertainty coming to meet.
>> She approaches slowly.

The Superior Woman is tempted to act out of unclear passion. She analyzes her reasons for desire, and in better self-awareness she approaches. With caution she acts well and avoids hurt to herself and her Sister. In her uncertainty, she realizes she is out of her depths and waits for understanding. By coming to meet slowly and with consideration, she does and suffers no harm.

> *Nine in the fourth line:*
>> No coming to meet.
>> No error.

The Superior Woman makes no move that is unwelcome to her lover. She waits for agreement or she does not act. By respecting one another, coming to meet brings the Sisters no blame.

> *Nine in the fifth place:*
>> Coming to meet in order.
>> Supreme blessings.

The Superior Woman protects her lover in caring and gentleness, and her lover protects her in turn. They come to meet in the perfections of the gentle wind and the universe. They are yin and yang dualities that form a whole.

> *Nine at the top:*
> A woman chooses celibacy.
> Continuing flow.

A Sister in matriarchy chooses to refuse coming to meet, and takes no lover. She has been hurt and needs a time of healing, a time of space and freedom for awhile; she is fulfilled and completed alone. Though judged different or arrogant in her matriarchy, the Superior Woman remains correct. She chooses her path and changes when she meets her times of change. In following this aspect of universal harmony, she finds affirmation and peace.

45. TS'UI / GATHERING TOGETHER

Above: Tui – The Joyous Daughter, Lake

Below: K'un – The Pentacle, Earth

Ts'ui remembers Hexagram 8, *Holding Together*. In the earlier hexagram, the chalice, water is above the pentacle, and in *Ts'ui* the lake is above the earth. Water gathers to fill a lake, and *Gathering Together* is the gathering of many women, as opposed to *Pi*'s union of two. Therefore, this hexagram refers to the gathering together of women into matriarchy.

THE CENTER – Women Gather Together. Matriarchy Grows.

> Gathering together
> Into matriarchy.
> Empowerment on the
> Wheel of Life.

Women gathering together is a natural spiral, whether the gathering be of two lovers, of women and their Daughters in a family, or of Sisters in the gathering of matriarchy. Spirituality circles, work sharings, gatherings at night to sing beside a campfire, and gatherings together for the sharing of meals are other types of gatherings in women's lives. Each Sister leads in some type of gathering together; all women are leaders in the matriarchy.

By women's communal spirituality and respect, by caring for each other, matriarchy is made strong and indissolvable. By inner awareness and attunement to the earth as Goddess, and the Wheel of Life, the women of matriarchy are gathered and united.

REFLECTION

> The lake over earth:
> Gathering together.
> Women gather and
> Matriarchy flows.

Lakewater rises till she flows beyond her banks: the matriarchy flows to become the tides of time. Women gather together to live and love, to work and share and heal. In mutual caring and respect is the strength and triumph of matriarchy. In her nurturing climate, women are prepared for obstacles and dangers; they face them and prevail in peace.

MOVEMENT

> *Six at the beginning:*
> They ask for grounding
> Gathered together.

The women gather together for a first meeting on the new moon. They do not know each other and hesitate to trust. The Sisters are uncentered and unfocused; they are not unified, but know what they wish to build. Gathered into a circle, the women ask for oneness and grounding. They ask for healing, sharing and openness. By their honesty and sincerity the Goddess blesses them. They are not denied her gifts.

Six in the second line:
>   They are attracted together.
>   Open affirmations.

In gathering together, women are led to correctness. They feel attraction for like-minded Sisters, and a need together to unify the matriarchy. Working as one inside this compelling attraction, yielding to her gladly, the women accept each other quickly and well. The work of building the matriarchy is begun from within, and open affirmations result.

Six in the third position:
>   She gathers together late.
>   She enters.

A woman wishes to enter the craft, but the circle is closed to newcomers. She joins an outer circle and she studies and waits, participating however she can. In matriarchy, no woman is ignored or excluded; the Superior Woman enters and is welcomed at last.

Nine in the fourth place:
>   Gathering together.
>   Great good.

The Superior Woman gathers her Sisters together in a common cause. She does not seek self-reward, but acts in the voice of women's unity for the good of all. Women recognize her efforts and they lend her their skills. Together they achieve the strength and triumph of matriarchy.

Nine in the fifth line:
>   She gathers her Sisters.
>   No error.

While all women are leaders and workers in matriarchy, a Mother rises in purpose among them. By her skills and common sense, by her wisdom and ability to give and receive, the Sisters respect her and love her. The Sisters look to the Superior Woman for guidance, and she gives them her best. With a Mother's honesty and integrity, the Superior Woman facilitates for the good of all.

Six at the top:
>   Gathering together.
>   She endures.

The Superior Woman wants to work with a Sister, but the Sister does not recognize her skills. The Superior Woman focuses on agreement and understanding, and her Sister grows in awareness. By her persistence and her Sister's acceptance, the matriarchy gains. Each woman has something to offer her circle. In offering what she can, the Superior Woman achieves progress and her matriarchy gathers together.

46. SHÊNG / THE TREE OF LIFE (REACHING)

Above: K'un — The Pentacle, Earth

Below: Sun — The Gentle Wind/Wood

Shêng is the Tree of Life, the effort of growing and reaching that brings achievement. Wood, the lower trigram, reaches through the earth above her. Growth extends from the center and rises to attain the stars.

The Hopi call the spruce tree the Tree of Life, and name her Salavi. She is honored yearly in the Niman Kachina ceremonies at summer solstice. Salavi brings rain, the source of life; her branches are the throne of the clouds. The spirit of Salavi, the clouds she reaches for, and the rain she brings to earth are a cycle in the Wheel of the universe.*

THE CENTER — The Tree of Life. She Reaches and Achieves.

> The Tree of Life.
> Reaching.
> She exceeds her grasp.

---

*Frank Waters, *Book of the Hopi*, (New York, Ballantine Books, 1963), p. 247.

A tree grows upward through earth, and her leaves gain the sky and universe. Her roots remain firmly below. The Priestess of matriarchy reaches in the way of the tree and achieves; with hard work and thoughtful choices, she attains her goals, and is connected to the earth and stars. In a time of effort and action, with her roots deeply strong and her branches proud and high, a Priestess and Spiritual Woman achieves beyond her dreams.

REFLECTION

> The tree reaches
> Through earth:
> The Priestess
> Grows connected.

The tree grows upward from earth to sky, and her roots are firm and strong underground. She reaches steadily and gains slowly; without speed she takes no pause. The Priestess is as steady and sure as the Tree of Life; she never stops in her confidence or striving.

MOVEMENT

> *Six at the beginning:*
> Reaching early.
> She gains courage.

As growth starts, the Priestess draws nourishment from her beginnings. Her strength comes from the deepest of her roots, her spiritual base. Like the Tree of Life, a Priestess of matriarchy is the earth and the universe. She has the courage to reach out and grow.

> *Nine in the second position:*
> Over-reaching.
> She learns.

The Priestess over-extends her reach. She wishes to do well and is firm in her efforts, but the task is beyond her growth. This is a compromising situation, but the Priestess and Spiritual Woman asks for help. She approaches her Mothers and Sisters in matriarchy and they lend her support and aid. The task is completed successfully, and the Priestess learns a boundary of her present reach.

Nine in the third line:
>She reaches for stars.
>No obstacles.

Obstacles disappear, and the Priestess reaches to gain her dreams. She grows with her progress and offers thanks, but remembers the law of change. She celebrates her prosperity as given and enjoys herself while she may.

Six in the fourth place:
>She reaches for others,
>And is recognized.

The Priestess reaches high for her matriarchy, and gives greatly from her possessions and inward skills. Her Sisters realize her contributions and her reachings, and choose to honor her in the circle. By recognition of her growth and attainments, they praise the Goddess as well.

Six in the fifth line:
>Continuing growth.
>Good reaching.

The Priestess of matriarchy gains in her reaching, but is not overwhelmed by prosperity. Her gifts are from the Goddess and she channels them to all. By strong and continuing growth, by gradual learning and action with connectedness to her roots, the Priestess gains progress. Endurance is her means to good reaching.

Six at the top:
>Reaching inward.
>The Tree of Life.

To succeed in reaching, to make achievements that are lasting and good, the Priestess and Spiritual Woman know when to proceed and when not to. Progress is not always a straight line, and she who reaches without inner awareness fails. Like the life of the Tree, progress and reaching are upward and downward, participating in all of the contradictions at once. By continuing and endurance, by steady and unremitting work at reaching, the Priestess achieves growth and gains affirmations of her goals.

47. K'UN / DEPLETION

Above: Tui — The Joyous Daughter, Lake

Below: K'an — The Chalice, Water

The upper trigram is the lake, but her waters are below her. Her chalice of fullness and nourishment is depleted and the lake bed is dry. Depletion and burnout dominate for the moment; after filling there is emptying in the Wheel of Life. Once the bottom of the chalice is reached, the lake fills again.

A woman's cycles follow the courses of the moon. As the moon reaches her full, wanes to darkness and then waxes again, a woman's womb waxes and empties in her menstrual cycle. Her lunar pattern of filling and emptying follows the Wheel of Life. Moon blood and the moon's dark phases are sacred times, times of power and magick. Emptying and depletion in this hexagram are preparations for refilling fulfillment.

THE CENTER — Depletion. She Chooses Fullness.

> Depletion and emptying.
> The Superior Woman
> Chooses fullness.
> And refills.

Depletion is the opposite of Hexagram 46, *Reaching*, but the Superior Woman meets and changes her. She is not overcome by trial or misfortune. She remains calm and connected to the Wheel of Life, and reverses and fulfills to success.

REFLECTION

>Water under the lake:
>Depletion.
>The Superior Woman
>Fills clear and strong.

Water has left the lake and the lake is depleted and empty; a time of challenge and trial is at hand. The Superior Woman does not allow depletion to defeat her. She creates her fate by free will. Her integrity and optimism are strong, and her faith is clear and enlightened. The Superior Woman fulfills her path and turns her life around.

MOVEMENT

>*Six at the beginning:*
>Under trial,
>She is depleted.
>Three long years.

In a phase of trial, the Superior Woman fills from within; if she lets go of her groundedness and affirmation, she depletes her source. She walks beneath the powerful dark moon without recognizing her gifts, and in her depression, she takes no control of her fate. The Superior Woman is a woman who fights back.

>*Nine in the second place:*
>She is depleted
>Though full.
>She offers her skills.

The Superior Woman is depressed and withdrawn, depleted by a rut of daily living that sucks her dry. She has gained prosperity but starves within, and sees no fulfillment in sight. The matriarchy is in need of Superior Women, and she offers her skills in sharing. The time is early and tenuous, but she reaches for affirmations and is fulfilled.

>*Six in the third position:*
>The Superior Woman
>Is not depleted.
>She is strong.

The Superior Woman does not find depletion in fullness, nor does she cause depletion by acting against universal harmony. She depends on certainties and not on shifting sands, yet is part of the Wheel of change and life. The Superior Woman acts decisively and knows why she acts. By her courage and centeredness in times of challenge and depletion, she refills and directs her fate.

Nine in the fourth line:
She fills too slowly,
And with low self-esteem.
No depletion in the end.

A woman recognizes a need she tries to fill, but is timid and indecisive in the means. She begins too slowly and is hindered in her task. By her insecurity, she follows instead of leads, and cannot move forward or backward. Her intent is clear and good, however, and delays are only temporary. She takes charge and acts in the end, and fulfills her goals.

Nine in the fifth place:
She is depleted
In influence.
Filling furthers.

The Superior Woman has honest intentions and a clear view, but cannot convince her Sisters. In confronting the Mothers and Priestesses of her matriarchy, she finds no accord and is depleted. For now, the Superior Woman withdraws into herself. Until the time of fulfillment, she finds comfort from within.

Six at the top:
She is depleted
By uncertainty.
Fullness later.

The Superior Woman is depleted by past failures. Her troubles and blockages are over, but she is not yet aware this is so. Once she understands her changed position, she redefines her goals: she affirms her present and future and releases her past. The Superior Woman acts from her new positivity and fills with clarity and light. Fullness arises from her choices.

48. CHING / THE WELL

▬▬ ▬▬	
▬▬▬▬▬	*Above:* K'an — The Chalice, Water
▬▬ ▬▬	
▬▬▬▬▬	
▬▬▬▬▬	*Below:* Sun — The Gentle Wind/Wood
▬▬ ▬▬	

The trigram for water rises above the trigram for wood. A Tree of Life draws water from the ground, and raises her above the source. She draws nourishment through her roots, through her trunk and leaves, releasing her into the sky. In a well, wood from the tree lines a tunnel dug into earth; the well becomes a chalice holding water, the cup of nourishment brought to women's lips. In ancient China, water was drawn from wells in clay buckets, and hauled to the surface by wooden poles. The well is spirituality and inner knowledge, the Goddess' abundance of life.

THE CENTER — The Well. She is There for All.

> The source is unfailing.
> Women gather at the well.
> Nourishment is there for all.

The well, where women draw water for drinking and cooking, for washing and agriculture, is the center of matriarchal society. Women go to her for life's nourishment, for the nourishments of spirituality and women's community. Sisters meet at her rim, and the wellspring is unfailing in her gifts.

In matriarchy, women drink of the sources of life. The need for inner harmony is recognized and sustained and no Sister's thirst is unquenched. The Superior Woman draws certainty from the well of herstory, from her Sisters' and Mothers' experiences and her own. She is nourished by learning, spirituality and the clarity of intuition. Her skills are the nourishment of matriarchy, connected to the Goddess' source.

REFLECTION

> Water above wood:
> The well.
> The Sisters nourish
> Matriarchy.

The roots of the Tree of Life bring water from the earth, and the tree in her growth functions as a living well. All that exists is nurtured by water rising over wood. In matriarchy as in the image of the well, women work to nourish their world.

MOVEMENT

> *Six at the beginning:*
> She does not drink
> From the well.
> She thirsts.

A woman refuses her clear connection with the source, and loses her way to the well. She is thirsty but her Sisters cannot help her. She walks in deserts until she returns to her beginnings. Lost to spirituality and matriarchy, she travels alone till she learns.

> *Nine in the second place:*
> The well is
> Undiscovered.
> Matriarchy thirsts.

The well is pure but undiscovered, and the matriarchy thirsts. Crops fail and Daughters suffer; the Sisters have nothing to drink. By not utilizing the Superior Woman's spirituality and skills, by not recognizing the source of her power, the matriarchy struggles unnourished.

> *Nine in the third line:*
> The well is known
> But not drunk from.
> Great sadness.

The well is discovered but women do not drink from her; the Superior Woman's skills and spirituality are unused. This situation is a sadness and waste of resources in matriarchy. When her Sisters recognize and draw upon her, all gain.

Six in the fourth position:
>   The Wisewoman
>   Seeks the well.
>   Future good.

A Wisewoman withdraws for awhile from matriarchy. She seeks knowledge of the mysteries of the well of life, and chooses to work in solitude. Her learning is benefit in potential. When she returns to the flow of the matriarchy, she is clearer and more skilled, and has grown in depth and strength. Her Sisters gain from her teaching.

Nine in the fifth line:
>   The clear well
>   Nourishes.
>   Pure flowing.

A pure well sustains life and is the source of life, and the Superior Woman is like the purest well. She is a chalice of crystal clarity and a Mother in matriarchy. Her skills and spirituality are respected, sought and utilized; they are a source of matriarchal power. The Superior Woman is a model for her Sisters; she flows and nourishes all.

Six at the top:
>   Women meet
>   At the well.
>   Bright blessings.

All who approach the well are nourished and no woman leaves thirsty. Her abundance is there for all. Water rises from the earth and women receive her. The Superior Woman is part of the Goddess, a limitless well, a source of nourishment for herself and her matriarchy. The more she gives, the more the Superior Woman has to give; she is blessed and a source of blessings, and she flows.

49. KO / CHANGE AND TRANSFORMATIONS

Above: Tui — The Joyous Daughter, Lake

Below: Li — The Wand, Fire

The trigrams are fire and water, conflicting elements that cannot mix or merge, and change is the result of their meeting. The Superior Woman realizes the inevitable necessity of change and transformations, for without them comes no growth. She chooses how change affects her destiny and fate by her actions within them. In each step taken or decisions made, transformations occur. They are part of the Wheel of Life, to be flowed with and not resisted, and implicit in the nature of the spiral. Like the Hanged One card in the Tarot, a reading of *Ko* in *The Kwan Yin Book of Changes* reflects endings and beginnings in process. With spirituality and connectedness, the Superior Woman emerges better and stronger for the changes she undergoes.

THE CENTER — Change in Her Time. She Grows.

> Change and transformations:
> In her time,
> She achieves
> Growth and peace.

Change is a conflict of necessities and a serious time, but change and transformations are the beginnings and endings of the Wheel. The Superior Woman proceeds from one cycle to the next; something ends and something rebegins. She flows with her changes and directs them. In matriarchy, in relationships, and within her inner self, transformations are at hand. Despite the period of upheaval, peace and growth emerge.

REFLECTION

> Fire over water:
> Change and transformations.
> The Superior Woman
> Follows her Wheel.

Times change and with them life changes. The seasons travel the Wheel of the Year, of the centuries. Transformation is reflected in the cycles of matriarchy and her women. Maiden becomes Mother becomes Crone in her time. The Superior Woman does not resist these transformations, but notes their natures and learns to adapt. She works within the spiral to choose and act in free will. She finds order in apparent chaos and achieves peace.

MOVEMENT

> *Nine at the beginning:*
> Early changes.
> She is centered.
> No error.

Changes occur at the breaking points of necessities, and are not easy times. In their beginning confusions, the Superior Woman moves slowly and carefully. She walks centered in the cycles of the earth and universe, and waits for her time to act.

> *Six in the second line:*
> Transformations
> In matriarchy.
> Beginning actions.

Transformation in matriarchy is near; the time is inevitable and the Sisters are ready. The Superior Woman accepts change and works for and within her. She begins to take action, and her actions are thoughtful and good. The matriarchy gains in strength by her flowing.

> *Nine in the third position:*
> Three times
> In the circle.
> There is change.

In a time of change, the women proceed cautiously but decisively, and thought-through analysis is not ignored. When an issue circles the matriarchy on three separate occasions and is finally agreed upon by consensus, the Superior Woman follows her Sisters into change.

Nine in the fourth line:
>   The Superior Woman
>   Supports
>   Good changes.

Changes in matriarchy occur by consensus of the Sisters. The Superior Woman and her community work for change through spiritual development and connectedness to the Wheel of Life and the Goddess. When change is for the gain and benefit of all, there is process and success. The Superior Woman supports changes that bring good.

Nine in the fifth place:
>   She walks brightly
>   And wins her
>   Sister's support.

In transformations, the Superior Woman is aware of her inner principles, within which she knows how to act. By walking bright and correct paths, she wins her Sisters' support.

Six at the top:
>   One thing
>   Becomes another.*
>   She endures.

After great transformations, smaller details also change. The Superior Woman realizes how much change is possible at this time, and does not apply undue pressures. New changes are made on the bases of the old, on what has already gone before. She builds her changes slowly to accumulate and grow.

---

*Principle wiccan saying. In Starhawk, *The Spiral Dance: A Rebirth of the Ancient Religion of the Great Goddess*, (San Francisco, Harper and Row Publishers, 1979), p. 171.

50. TING / THE CAULDRON

Above: Li — The Wand, Fire

Below: Sun — The Gentle Wind/Wood

Ting is the Cauldron of Ceridwen, composed of the trigrams fire over wood. Like her complement, Hexagram 48, *The Well*, she illustrates a woman-made object, a symbol that is both earthly and universal in qualities of nourishment and emergence. Where the well nourishes matriarchy, and her water is the beginning source of life, the cauldron or cooking pot nourishes the spirit and represents birth, death and transformation.

When women gather in a circle, the Cauldron of Ceridwen is their center. She is Hecate and Morrigan, the dark moon, the Crone, the focal point of reincarnation and change. She is essence beyond the four elements, the power to become. Women enter her to end and to begin, to die, to change and be reborn. The Hopi call her sipapu, the earth's womb, through which all travel to emerge and leave the world.

THE CENTER — The Cauldron of Ceridwen. The Wheel.

> She changes
> Everything She touches,
> And everything She touches
> Changes.*

The cauldron is a three-legged bronze cooking pot that rests on a wood fire. In the Chinese temple, she represents the foremothers, and food cooked in her is served to participants of ritual. As fire

---

*Principle wiccan waying. In Starhawk, *The Spiral Dance: A Rebirth of the Great Goddes*, (San Francisco, Harper and Row Publishers, 1979), p. 67.

transforms vegetables and herbs into nourishing soup, death and rebirth transform the spirit and are the center of the Wheel of Life and her mysteries. Her symbol of the cauldron reaches between the worlds and illustrates cosmic law. An understanding of the Cauldron of Ceridwen is clarity, certainty and peace.

REFLECTION

> Flame beyond wood:
> The Cauldron of Ceridwen.
> The Superior Woman
> Emerges and transforms.

Fire burns by air and wood, and wood is earth and water: the four elements interact. With fuel and fire below her, the cauldron cooks and nourishes. Life too, is a Wheel of forces and elements, a circle of changes and power in beginnings and endings. The Superior Woman understands this circle and her part in her, accepts and directs her place on the Wheel of Life, and learns the secret of inner peace.

MOVEMENT

> *Six at the beginning:*
> The Daughter emerges
> And is received.

Every Daughter has her place within matriarchy. She banishes her uncertainties and approaches the Mothers who welcome her. Despite her newness, the Daughter offers her skills, and her skills grow as she matures. She gains the respect and teachings of her Mothers and Sisters, and emerges and unfolds into light.

> *Nine in the second line:*
> Her Sisters disbelieve
> But do not fault her.

A Daughter directs her dreams and emergence towards the good of her world. Her goals are beyond expectations of what she can do. The Daughter is received with reservation by her Sisters, but with her good intent she wins acceptance. Her inexperience and innocence are protected and supported.

Nine in the third place:
    The Daughter emerges
    And is recognized.
A Daughter has psychic skills that are unrealized by her Sisters.
Her emergence and growth are unrecognized and untrained. In her
beginning spirituality and connectedness, she is discovered by a Mother
who teaches and guides her. The Daughter learns and gains direction,
and her skills are developed and used.

Nine in the fourth position:
    She tries but fails.
    She is young.
The Daughter faces a challenge beyond her strength and skills.
She misapplies her powers, and by over-confidence she does not ask
for help. Her Sisters are displeased with her; her Mothers wait. The
Daughter is still young and new.

Six in the fifth place:
    The Daughter seeks
    The Mothers' knowledge.
The Mothers are there to help the Daughter, and by asking for
help, the Daughter grows in strength and understanding. With temperate guides, the Daughter learns temperance and balance. She is praised
for her learning and supported in her efforts. Her knowledge grows
and changes, and her wisdom gains. She and her matriarchy benefit.

Nine at the top:
    She achieves higher levels.
    Blessed be.
In the fifth line of this hexagram, the Daughter accepts the
Mothers as her guides. In the top line, she merges their strength
with her own shining. She opens to the Goddess, and her Sisters
and Mothers help her to grow. The Mothers bring her to harmony
and belonging. Gentle and bright in her emerging and changing,
her Sisters support and welcome her. Matriarchy is built on her
Daughter's skills and warmed by her presence. Blessed be.

51. CHÊN / AWAKENING

———— ————
————————   *Above:* Chên — The Awakening, Thunder

———— ————
————————   *Below:* Chên — The Awakening, Thunder

The trigram *Chên* is repeated in this hexagram and is the thunder-shock of awakening awareness. An unbroken yang line under two shortened yin lines shows movement that is outward and positive. Emotion aroused by the awakening of women's spirituality is strong and opening. No skill is given that cannot be used for good, and a Daughter awakens to learning and psychic growth. With her arousal, she releases her potential for healing and empowerment. She connects with her matriarchy, and learns skills that bind her to the community. She uses her power for the good of all and is welcomed and celebrated. Awakening is a gift of the Goddess, a beginning, that is symbolized well by the thunder.

THE CENTER — She Awakens Spiritually. Great Joy.

> Awakening.
> The Daughter learns
> Inner awareness.
> She is blessed.

Awakening comes from the Goddess and comes as a shock. The power is great and unknown, but the Daughter's stress is not misfortune. She asks help of her Mothers and Priestesses, and they are there for her. In gentleness, the Daughter learns to use and respect her gifts. She becomes a healer at the Mothers' hands. The Daughter learns strength, control and caring, and to use her skills wisely and with joy.

REFLECTION

Thunder twice:
Awakening.
The Daughter looks within.

The Daughter awakens to the immanence of the Goddess, and finds her place on earth. She is filled with love and respect; she learns connectedness and seeks understanding. With good intent, she opens to new psychic skills. Her awakening changes her life and puts her in tune with the universe.

MOVEMENT

Nine in the first line:
Awakening starts.
She begins.
The shock of awakening comes so strongly that the Daughter is overwhelmed. Her fear is brief, however, as she begins to understand. She learns empowerment, what skills are within her, and how to use them for herself and her matriarchy. With help of her Mothers and Sisters, she grows confident, competent and secure.

Six in the second place:
Awakening with stress.
No error.
The shock of awakening rocks her stability for awhile. Great changes cause great reactions, and the Daughter seeks to act. She does not block the arousal of her powers, or resist her place on the Wheel of Life. She accepts her changes and seeks to understand. When initial stress ends, the Daughter is taught by the Mothers and Priestesses. She gains firmer stability than before.

Six in the third line:
Awakening unsettles her.
She learns action.
In the beginning of awakening, a Daughter resists; she loses self-confidence and hesitates to act. When she relaxes and flows with her changes, she takes her place in matriarchy and assumes control of her life. This is the meaning of awakening and empowerment.

Nine in the fourth position:
Awakening falters.
Temporary blockage.

Awakening occurs when her time is right, and outer events do not prevent or halt her. A Daughter makes her gentlest growth, however, with the help of a guide. Her guide is within or without, but a Mother of matriarchy teaches the Daughter well. Until a Mother is found, the Daughter falters temporarily. She comes to no harm in her period of waiting; the Goddess protects her and the universe lends her strength.

Six in the fifth place:
She awakens
And is centered.

In a time of continuing shock and arousal, the Daughter experiences great stress. She is not in peril and comes to no harm, but eventually attains centeredness. No longer unsettled by the storms of her new awareness, she grows in understanding and recognizes her place on the Wheel of Life. The Mothers and Priestesses encourage her as she learns.

Six at the top:
Awakening action.
She flows.

In her time of awakening and emergence, the Daughter loses herself for awhile, but regains herself and her powers tenfold. In the beginning, she is afraid to use her new skills. Once she gains centering and finds a Mother to teach her, she is ready again to act. The universe protects a Daughter from harm while she is learning. Her intent is good, and her actions proceed on good paths. The Daughter becomes a Superior Woman, with power to heal herself and the earth.

52. KÊN / CENTERING (CONNECTING)

```
—— ——
—— ——
```
Above: Kên – Keeping Still, Mountain

```
—— ——
—— ——
```
Below: Kên – Keeping Still, Mountain

The hexagram repeats the trigram *Kên*, and *Keeping Still* is her Chinese name. The symbol is a union of polarities, of active and receptive principles. Movement unwinds naturally to a place of quiet peace. In the Spiritual Woman, keeping still is called connecting or centering. A clear mind begins the process of awareness, the stillness that soars within. Keeping still is a connecting with the earth, and with all that lives on the planet; she is a connecting with the Goddess who is the earth. As in Hexagram 46, *The Tree of Life*, "we feel how beneath the earth all our roots entwine, how they draw power from the same source. And we feel above our heads how our branches entwine, how the same wind moves through them all".* This centering is the point from which spiritual work is raised. She is a state of calm clarity, a polarity and flight of stillness from which movement rebegins.

THE CENTER – Centering. She Touches the Earth and the Stars.

> Centering.
> She touches Goddess.
> Peace.

The Spiritual Woman learns stillness within, connection to the Goddess and her inner self. From the center begins her flight of awareness, and she begins from knowledge that all life is one. The Goddess is immanence; she not only makes the earth, but she *is* the earth. With relatedness to her roots, the Spiritual Woman connects all life to her

---

*Starhawk, *Dreaming the Dark: Magic, Sex and Politics*, (Boston, Beacon Press, 1982), p. 31.

own participation in life. She achieves stillness from this center, a oneness with the source, and becomes part of the perfection of the universe.

Centering means action from a solid base and thought from a place of clarity. She is stillness in times of waiting, and decision and motion in times of moving ahead. The Spiritual Woman acts from an awareness that each ending is a new beginning, and actions from her center change the world.

REFLECTION

> Mountains as one:
> Centering.
> The Spiritual Woman
> Connects to her source.

Mountains reach into sky and into earth, and partake of both in their natures. Together they are one connected base. Thoughts too, are connected essences, reaching into sky and ground. The Spiritual Woman flies her thoughts with relatedness to her planet and all life. She flies them within harmonies of the Goddess, and is part of the Goddess' universe. By her connectedness, she empowers herself, and respects and benefits all that lives.

MOVEMENT

> *Six at the beginning:*
> She seeks centering.
> And opens her wings.

When she first starts learning to center, the Spiritual Woman does not connect easily. Her newness is a place of her own, and she does not know what she lacks or seeks. By good intent in her everyday actions and by continuing and reaching out with openness, she spreads her wings and finds her way.

> *Six in the second place:*
> She flies forward.
> Good beginnings.

The Spiritual Woman lights a silver candle to visualize the Lady. She focuses on flame, and holds stillness in her mind for an instant.

Though she loses her connection quickly, she has seen. She tries again and flies forward. That she gains the feeling of being centered at all is a good start.

   Nine in the third position:
      She forces flight
      And sees nothing.
   The woman glimpses a moment of centeredness, but does not know how to regain her. She stares into distances with her intellect, not her intuition, and tries in vain to force herself to connect. Stillness comes only easily and naturally. The Spiritual Woman has not yet found her way to centeredness, but centeredness approaches. In the meantime, she learns to fly gently.

   Six in the fourth line:
      She centers with her Sisters.
      And stretches her wings.
   The Spiritual Woman finds moments of centeredness, but does not achieve her at will. She comes to a circle of women and asks to join. The women accept her and a Mother guides her. They do meditations together and the woman relaxes into stillness. In her state of connected awareness, the flight of centering comes.

   Six in the fifth place:
      She learns to center.
      She flies.
   The Spiritual Woman learns to ground and center. She protects herself, enters rapport with the earth, and finds peace. Once she discovers connectedness, she finds her at will. As she does, her centering is natural and in tune. Her heart is at rest and her thoughts are still. She reaches new inner levels, and learns the meaning of flight.

   Nine at the top:
      She is centered
      And flies swiftly.
   The Spiritual Woman sees herself as part of the earth and universe. She is the Goddess, and the Goddess is within her and without. The Spiritual Woman is in tune with the harmonies of the life force. She is quiet and at peace within, and discovers empowerment. The Spiritual Woman flies swiftly and begins her quest.

53. CHIEN / DEVELOPMENT (GROWTH)

Above: Sun — The Gentle Wind/Wood

Below: Kên — Keeping Still, Mountain

The hexagram pictures the Tree of Life on a still mountain, and is comprised of the trigrams *Sun* and *Kên*. A tree grows in her own way and time; she develops quietly and surely, sending her roots deep into earth and her branches to the sky. By participation in the balance of nature, the tree becomes strong and secure. *Chien* also indicates stillness and perception, an absence of haste and heedless activity that is required for development to occur.

THE CENTER — Development. She Grows Slowly and Well.

> Development.
> She grows in
> Inner strength.

The Tree of Life grows slowly and deeply, as does the growth of any real learning or relationship. The Superior Woman develops inner spirituality and grows in skills. Her awareness increases steadily and without haste in her time. In relationships too, the Superior Woman allows respect to gain, and develops trust and openness gradually. Her development is full and continuing, and comes from within.

REFLECTION

> A tree on the mountain:
> Development.
> The Superior Woman
> Grows in respect.

A tree grows slowly over many years and changes, and the ancient Crone tree on a mountaintop is a magick force. The effort of spiritual development occurs as slowly and surely as the Tree of Life — she does not happen overnight. In matriarchy too, the power of a Superior Woman grows deeply and from a firm base. By the slow growth of inner development, the Superior Woman gains respect in her relationships and community.

MOVEMENT

Six at the first line:
> She begins to develop
> And is welcomed.

A woman enters the matriarchy. She does not know anyone or her way is slow to begin, but her Sisters welcome her. Her skills are needed and she is not a stranger for long. The Superior Woman is careful in her actions and grows in respect; her Mothers and Sisters help her to develop. Every woman has a place in matriarchy.

Six in the second position:
> A warm place.
> She grows strong.

The Superior Woman develops warmly in matriarchy, and her growth is supported and increased. She hesitates less and her way is open to action; she responds to affirmations with confidence and joy. In her growing self-worth and skills, the Superior Woman is able to give of her self.

Nine in the third place:
> She loses the Wheel.
> Temporary lack of growth.

A woman loses the Wheel of Life and by excess goes astray. This is a temporary misfortune. The Superior Woman lets relationships grow slowly and in their time; to force them violates cosmic law. In her development, the Superior Woman holds to her integrity and does not deny her inner self. By knowing when to wait, she regains the Wheel, and grows from her mistakes as from her triumphs.

Six in the fourth line:
> A tenuous development.
> No error.

The Superior Woman finds herself in a tenuous position, and is there through error or inexperienced judgment. She thinks things out before she acts. By awareness she finds a new refuge, or a light at the end of the tunnel. No process of development is obstacle-free.

Nine in the fifth place:
Alienation and error.
Eventual development.

The Superior Woman is respected in matriarchy but holds herself aloof from her Sisters. She is misunderstood because she sets herself apart. No woman is greater than another in matriarchy, though greater skills bring larger responsibilities. No goals are achieved in isolation. The Superior Woman offers her skills and works in harmony with her Sisters. She grows and continues to develop.

Nine at the top:
Development through life.
Continuing growth.

The Superior Woman develops in awareness and learning throughout her life. She is curious and perceptive in her seeking and accepts growth from every action and situation she meets. The Superior Woman learns from her Daughters and Sisters, from her Mothers, Priestesses and Wisewomen. She listens to the earth and to herself as part of the universe, and grows daily to give of what she gains.

54. KUEI MEI / LIVING TOGETHER

Above: Chên – The Awakening, Thunder

Below: Tui – The Joyous Daughter, Lake

The trigrams are *Chên* and *Tui*, the awakening thunder and joyous lake. Two women awakening into love for each other, into joy and a life of flowing as one, come together to begin a home. This is a time of great and glad changes in the Sisters' lives. Lovers living together share and learn about each other, and each learning and day are new. Some times may be stormy, as shown by the thunder, but lovers merge with peace as the waters of a lake. When two women of matriarchy recognize their love, loneliness ends for both. In their undertaking of building a home, love and respect are achieved.

THE CENTER — Living Together. Bright Blessings.

> Living together.
> Two women make a home.
> They are blessed.

Lovers choose to live together, and find a place to make their home. They seek their living space, and the seeking together is their beginning and joy. They make preparations and move; their books are together on their own home's shelves. The lovers awaken in the mornings in a home of their own, and the first thing they see is each other. Together they begin, and their gladness and loving overflow.

REFLECTION

> Thunder and joy:
> Lovers live together.
> They continue in love.

Thunder and joy awaken with flowing; lovers live together in new lives. A relationship between women is sensitive; but love overcomes all obstacles. Sisters who choose to live together do so in caring and joy, and blessings abound if they work for them. The lovers follow and lead. With awareness of each other's sensitivities and space, and with work, caring and gentle flowing, the lovers build a stable home. Their relationship continues in the love they share, and they live together for life.

MOVEMENT

> *Nine at the beginning:*
>> They choose to live together.
>> Caring and peace.

The time is right; two women who love each other choose to make a home. They approach the idea carefully, shyly, and each fears being turned away. The lovers are ready, however, and the idea is an awakening and a joy. In their love together, there is something new. The decision is another beginning, and a greater one, than they knew as a couple before. The time is good for both of them; in their flowing is caring and peace.

> *Nine in the second line:*
>> She is lonely but waits.
>> No error.

Two Sisters who love each other are kept apart by distance or the circumstances of their work. They are lonely for each other, but though not often together, remain strong. The Superior Woman waits for her loneliness to end, and the lovers eventually live together. They build a life and a home when the time is good for both of them. The lovers wait in the meantime, are supportive of each other, and endure.

> *Six in the third place:*
>> They live together
>> For convenience.

Two Sisters whose lovers are far away or whose relationships are in flux, move in with each other. They are close friends but not lovers. Together they make a life, though each waits for her own love to return; they help and protect each other, and they share. The women are comfortable together, respect each other and are caring, but are not in love. Living together as roommates is no error. Time holds changes to come for both.

> *Six in the fourth position:*
>> The Superior Woman
>> Waits and endures.

Two women who love each other cannot live together; they are separated by distance or each other's fear of being hurt. The Superior Woman chooses to wait for her lover's return. She offers caring and endures. Her friends laugh and chide her for her faith; they fear she is misled. The Superior Woman holds to the one she knows loves her. She waits while waiting is needed, and the lovers live together at last.

Six in the fifth line:
> They live together
> Eventually.

Two women finally come together. They meet each other slowly, with fear of being hurt, but their hesitancy ends. They are open to one another, and flow together in the merging of true love. A time of uncertainty and loneliness for both is past; the lovers come together and live together, and their life as a couple begins. The joy of their meeting is an offering to the Goddess, and she smiles.

Six at the top:
> They live together daily.
> Bright blessings.

Two women who were apart find each other's love and begin a new home. They learn about each other everyday. They merge at night and hold each other, and together they find peace and joy. The Superior Woman does not lose her being in the being of her lover. She is a woman of her own thoughts and needs. Lovers live together in cherishing and respect, but are still individual women. Each day they are together brings them stronger and surer in love.

55. FÊNG / ABUNDANCE (FULLNESS)

Above: Chên — The Awakening, Thunder

Below: Li — The Wand, Fire

Awakening moves upward and flame is inner light: their result is

Robin Wood 1987

abundance and fullness, a height of prosperity, progress and success. She is a time of fulfillment, and of harvest in the year. In the Wheel of Life, fullness is followed by waning and change always comes. In the year, winter follows the abundance of gathering in. The season is Mabon, the fall equinox of September 22; she is Virgo and Libra in the zodiac, and Eusaumuya, the women's healing dances, in the Hopi calendar. Although waning follows fullness, *Fêng* is not an unfavorable hexagram. The emphasis here is on balance, abundance, prosperity and change.

THE CENTER — Full Abundance. A Time of Joy.

> Abundance and fullness.
> Prosperous heights.
> She triumphs in plenty.

Fullness is a time of pleasure and satisfaction, the harvesting of deeds. Though moments of height are temporary, the Superior Woman sees joy where she comes. She accepts her gifts as given and fully appreciates them. Her abundance comes from hard work and the conscious earning of skills. The Superior Woman rejoices in achievements and accepts her fullness in triumph.

REFLECTION

> Thunder and lightning:
> The image of abundance.
> The Superior Woman
> Recognizes light.

Chên is thunder, and *Li* is fire and lightning; the Superior Woman arouses her inner awareness. In the fullness of abundance, of awakened development and skills, she accepts a zenith of earned prosperity. Fullness is followed by waning, and the Superior Woman is also aware of changes. In the balance of natural harmonies in the universe, she follows the Wheel of Life.

MOVEMENT

> *Nine at the beginning:*
>> Abundant merging
>> And fullness.

Two Sisters in matriarchy who are active, aware and clear, meet and are drawn together. The time they take in learning from and about each other is abundant. They recognize the affinities and polarities in each other and forge the fullness of a bond. Benefit results from their merging.

> *Six in the second place:*
>> A lunar eclipse.
>> Hidden fullness.

In a time of disharmony, Sisters misunderstand each other and factions arise. The effect is of the moon hiding her face from the matriarchy. The Superior Woman knows that this is not a time for force. She waits for her Sisters to change, and they do, and her integrity continues in abundance. Harmony is regained, and the light of the Lady Moon returns.

> *Nine in the third line:*
>> A dark moon.
>> Waning conflict.

The time is dark, and the moon is hidden from the earth. After waning, however, she waxes again. The new moon is a time of potential and mystery in the fertile night. In matriarchy too, the Superior Woman faces times of obstacles and conflict. She does not lose her brightness of outlook, and all things change. She waxes to fullness in time.

> *Nine in the fourth position:*
>> The first quarter.
>> Advancing abundance.

Light waxes and the moon is a sliver of hope, a promise of returning abundance. Power is used with gentle correctness and wisdom by the Superior Woman. When action and understanding go together, she succeeds and gains in fullness.

Six in the fifth line:
   The full moon.
   Brightest abundance.
   In a time of energy and light, the women in joy honor darkness; they celebrate the esbat with a spiral dance. The Superior Woman takes advice from her Sisters and Mothers in matriarchy. She achieves new clarity and perspectives, and her decisions are fuller towards success. By reserve, integrity and caution, she achieves her goals and finds abundance in all her changes.

Six at the top:
   Hoarded abundance.
   The waning moon.
   The woman achieves abundance and prosperity, and holds onto her with both hands. She refuses to recognize change or her responsibility to share. The Superior Woman shares fullness and skills with her Sisters and matriarchy. By doing so, she grows in both. In setting her fullness apart and hoarding her prosperity, the Superior Woman does not halt change but hastens her. No time remains in stasis. By recognizing the Wheel of Life and the necessity of giving, the Superior Woman avoids error and waning.

56. LÜ / THE WANDERER

Above: Li – The Wand, Fire

Below: Kên – Keeping Still, Mountain

   A mountain waits, but flame moves quickly upward, the trigrams do not meet. A young woman chooses to live on the road. She leaves her community through restlessness or not knowing where to go, but carries her joy, pain and loneliness within. The Superior Woman seeks learning and spiritual peace by the roads she travels. She has freedom, and a mobility her Sisters envy, but does not lack inner or outer difficulties. She is the flame: her lover and matriarchy are mountains waiting at home.

THE CENTER — A Woman Seeks on the Roads. Rest in the End.

> The wanderer seeks
> On many paths.
> Eventually she comes home.

The Superior Woman who leaves her matriarchy to wander becomes strong and clear; her integrity protects her on the road. She reaches in openness to women she meets and they help her as they can. She offers her caring and help in return. Choosing to make no ties and lonely in her choice, the wanderer's lover and family wait. Eventually she returns to matriarchy, to a community she calls hers, and the growth and learning of her travels benefit in the end.

REFLECTION

> Flame over stillness:
> The wanderer.
> The Superior Woman
> Shines brightly.

A flaming wand does not remain still, and her light is seen from afar. The Superior Woman who lives on the road does not stay long in one place, but enlightens communities as she passes through them. Traveling brightly, a shooting star, she learns clarity, and brings clarity to all she meets.

MOVEMENT

> *Six at the beginning:*
> She wastes her skills
> And is incorrect.

The Superior Woman does not participate in activities that waste her time or skills. She makes no motions that harm herself or her Sisters, or that violate her inner principles. The woman who acts incorrectly faces peril. She recognizes her worth and finds and gives respect in all she does.

Six in the second line:
        She is welcomed
        And earns acceptance.
The Superior Woman is careful and gentle on the road. She remains connected with universal harmonies and the Goddess, and is in tune with Sisters who shelter her on her way. The peace and healing she radiates are recognized and welcomed, and the women she helps accept her in their homes. By her correctness, the Superior Woman finds help when she is in need.

Nine in the third place:
        The wanderer is not welcomed.
        Her Sisters err.
The wanderer stops at a woman's house but finds no admittance or shelter: her Sisters are gravely in error. Women help each other as they can. The wanderer offers skills in exchange for her lodgings, and her Sisters benefit from her presence. In things she has seen, the wanderer offers the women much. Women help other women in matriarchy; by this, bright blessings come to all.

Nine in the fourth position:
        She learns to let go.
        No error.
The Superior Woman chooses to go on the road, and takes few belongings with her. She learns to accept a lack of objects and comforts, and simplifies her needs and her life. Such letting go of the material is correct. She also chooses to let go of things of the spirit, of relationships and learning. In this case, great care is necessary to not withdraw from true needs.

Six in the fifth line:
        She works to change wrongs,
        And wrongs change.
The Superior Woman sees things that are wrong in her world, and participates in actions that change them. On the road, she has greater freedom to act in this manner. The woman who chooses to better her world, who puts herself and her integrity into helping things

change, changes herself and her community for the good. In matriarchy, women who work for such changes are respected and cherished.

> *Nine at the top:*
>> The Wheel of Change.
>> Bright blessings.

The Superior Woman builds her life on the Wheel of Changes. When she chooses to go on the road, she leaves her home and lover, and travels to learn what she needs. Once fulfilled, however, the Superior Woman recognizes her time to stop and find a home. With centeredness and inner awareness, and her ability to give and receive, she meets good fortune on her paths.

57. SUN / THE GENTLE

Above: Sun — The Gentle Wind/Wood

Below: Sun — The Gentle Wind/Wood

Sun is another of eight hexagrams in *The Kwan Yin Book of Changes* that repeats a basic trigram. Wind and wood are gentle strength, both receptive and discerning in their power. Nothing affects air with more energy than a gentle wind; no action affects earth with more power than a delicate root. Wind moves the clouds, clears the air, and the sky shines brightly with the stars and moon of peace. A root grows deeply to upthrust layers of rock. In the same way, the Spiritual Woman changes wrongs by her gentleness of integrity and perceptive light. The clarity and gentle awareness of Sisters too, make matriarchy strong. By the quality of gentle endurance every goal is achieved.

THE CENTER — The Gentle. Small Efforts Make Great Changes.

> The gentle.
> Small efforts
> Take hold firmly.
> And move the earth.

Gentleness achieves small-seeming gains that accumulate in power and strength. Increase is made by effort, not by force. Gentle attainments are subtle, develop quietly and grow gradually, but are strong, lasting and real. With clear destination and awareness, the Spiritual Woman finds gentle paths to her goals. Her actions take root slowly to move the earth.

REFLECTION

> Winds and woods playing:
> An image of gentleness.
> The Spiritual Woman
> Continues and achieves.

The powers of wind and wood come from gentle continuing motions. They do not stop or ever give up. Their strength is the ability to ignore time and take things as they come in actions that are gentle, slow and sure. Thorough goodness and gentleness affect matriarchy, as well. With ceaseless integrity, the Spiritual Woman uses them in her life to increase and benefit all.

MOVEMENT

> *Six at the beginning:*
> Indirection.
> She learns gentle certainty.

Gentleness carried to extremes is without direction or goals. Uncertainty dominates, and the Spiritual Woman is too confused to act. She casts herself to random winds and achieves nothing lasting or stable. By understanding and persistence, the Spiritual Woman learns and grows. She gains self-confidence and discipline, and her actions are both gentle and decisive.

Nine in the second place:
> Inner obstacles.
> Gentle confrontations.

The Spiritual Woman meets blocks to her goals, and they are obstacles from within. Gentle thoughts are overwhelming forces for decision or ambivalence. The Spiritual Woman traces her hindrances back to their root beginnings. They are elusive and seem ephemeral, but their confrontation is necessary for progress and empowerment.

Nine in the third position:
> Gentle thoughts.
> She triumphs.

The gentle power of inwardness is not carried beyond her time and place. To do so hinders decision and defuses power. The Spiritual Woman knows when she needs to act. There are times for thought and times for motion, and she is aware of the boundaries and consequences of each.

Six in the fourth line:
> Gentleness and action.
> She achieves.

Building on a series of gentle decisions, the Spiritual Woman acts towards enduring outcomes. By combining perception with energy and gentleness with movement, achievement is finally hers.

Nine in the fifth position:
> Gentle changes.
> The full moon.

Three days before and three days after the full moon: gentle steps are taken for change.* In every decision are actions and reactions that affect the Spiritual Woman and her matriarchy. When change is necessary, gentle deliberation first brings lasting gain and triumph. With gradual decisions and enduring actions, her future is assured and good.

Nine at the top:
> Gentle power.
> She prevails.

---

*Marion Weinstein, *Earth Magic: A Dianic Book of Shadows*, (Custer, WA, Phoenix Publishing Company, 1980), p. 35.

The Spiritual Woman learns that gentleness alone is not enough, and she backs her with power-from-within. Perception followed by good and timely actions brings real progress. The Spiritual Woman avoids force to gently reach her goals.

58. TUI / JOY

Above: Tui — The Joyous Daughter, Lake

Below: Tui — The Joyous Daughter, Lake

Tui is the last of eight hexagrams that doubles a basic trigram. She represents the Daughter who is safe and loved, and who is encouraged to grow into a Superior Woman of matriarchy. The Daughter's gentleness and overflowing happiness are grounded in certainty and her rising capable strength. She is a developing amazon nurtured and taught wisely to fulfill her limitless potential. True joy is adaptable and light, but issues from pools of inner courage and decision. She flows in relationships to more than the child. In the Tarot, *Tui* is the Ace of Cups, and the woman who draws her in a *Kwan Yin Book of Changes* reading is bathed in love and the joyful abundance of the nurturing Goddess.

THE CENTER — Joy. She Flows Brightly.

> Joy.
> The Lady's gifts.
> She flows in beauty.

The Superior Woman is positive and open, and her Sisters rejoice in her. As an emotion, joy is second in power only to love. When two women win each other's hearts, they win each other's respect and caring in joy as well. Joy is a wellspring of the Daughter present in the Superior Woman as an adult, and is a gift of the Goddess' great glowing.

REFLECTION

> Lakes lying together:
> There is joy.
> The Superior Woman
> Joins her Sisters and lover.

The waters of two lakes merge, and they fill each other by flowing together. This is the relationship between lovers or Sisters in matriarchy: their nurturing and caring helps them both to grow, and brings gladness and joy to their lives. Sisters or Daughters learn together, and their learning is a flowing of two streams. They vitalize each other, exchanging ideas and energies, and grow in new skills and strengths. As the Mother nourishes her Daughter and helps her to a space of exploration and freedom, so do lovers and Sisters nourish each other in joy. In any caring relationship — between lovers, friends, students, or Mother and Daughter — the quality of joy is fulfilled.

MOVEMENT

> *Nine in the beginning:*
> Inner joy.
> Flowing harmony.

The Superior Woman experiences joy from within. She has the inner certainty of centered peace that needs nothing from outside to sustain her. Such a woman knows freedom and strength, and is part of the flowing of the Goddess.

> *Nine in the second place:*
> Honest joys.
> Real pleasures.

The Superior Woman takes no joy from activities unworthy of her notice. She finds no gladness in things that demean or hurt her, and is not tempted by them. The Superior Woman lives by a higher strength and awareness that are always with her. This is reflected in her actions and desires, and brings her to find honest joy.

Six in the third line:
      Tinsel joy.
      She errs.
The woman is depleted of inner joy, and momentary pleasures seem real to her. She accepts the glitter not knowing her for false. The Superior Woman listens to her inner self and knows tinsel from genuine worth. She takes the superficial for empty outwardness, and looks further for true inner values.

Nine in the fourth position:
      The Daughter is joy.
      Gentle waters.
A Daughter of matriarchy is raised with gentleness. She is helped to a world of freedom and safety in which she explores and learns with joy. The Daughter flows in inner strength and peace: if she fails at times, she is not defeated, and most times she succeeds. She is always loved. Her growing is bathed in life as in nurturing waters, in connectedness to the Goddess and the earth.

Nine in the fifth line:
      Lovers.
      Flowing joy.
Two Sisters of matriarchy are lovers and beyond; they forge a relationship of mutual respect and trust. They care for, nurture and love each other, and their result is a sharing of joy and fulfillment. Their Ace of Cups overflows with gentle abundance, and the greatest of blessings is theirs.

Six at the top:
      They joy in learning.
      Good flowing.
Two women who are not lovers meet each other to learn. Together they explore ideas and spirituality, and together they learn new skills. Fulfillments of the intellect and psyche are joyful and nurturing: the Sisters reach great expansions. By reflecting their learnings with each other, the women reach perspectives they would not have reached alone. Their relationship of unity brings flowing joy.

59. HUAN / OPENING (DISPERSION)

Above: Sun — The Gentle Wind/Wood

Below: K'an — The Chalice, Water

Wind and wood are above the life source of water; the tree opens her roots to nourishment and growth. A woman of matriarchy opens herself to her Sisters: she disperses barriers that scatter her energy and breaks down distrusts that keep her isolated. By opening, the Superior Woman takes in life from the source. She disperses and dissolves her loneliness and lets go of fear.

THE CENTER — Opening. She Learns to Trust and She Grows.

> Opening.
> The Superior Woman
> Trusts her Sisters.

Huan is the opening and dispersion of fear, and tearing down walls is a force for greatest good. Spirituality brings women of matriarchy together, and teaches them skills of loving trust. When the Superior Woman opens to her Sisters, she tells them who she is. In her trust and sharing they comfort, support and protect her, and open to her in return. Through feelings, a woman dissolves the hardness of being alone, and openness puts her at one with the universe. When women open to each other in harmony with the Goddess and the earth, conflict and disunity are broken. Blockages disperse too, when the needs and nourishment of matriarchy are put first.

REFLECTION

> Wood and wind above water:
> Opening and dispersion.
> She dissolves to reunite.

Wind and wood rise above the trigram for water; opening and dispersion bring release and growth. In the minds of women, fear and suspicion create walls to be torn down. Isolation and blockages disperse to oneness and to trust. An opening to the harmonies of the Goddess is an opening to all women and all life. In unity and love the matriarchy prospers, and Sisters within her find peace.

MOVEMENT

Six at the beginning:
   She offers herself.
   Good opening.
Openness comes early in a relationship, if only in small ways. The Superior Woman offers help to a Sister in need; she offers her skills to any who wish to be aided. By offering help, the Superior Woman expresses her openness, and by accepting help, her Sister too, is opened. Thus with early openness, two women meet and establish a basis for trust.

Nine in the second position:
   She opens mistrust,
   And she wins.
The Superior Woman distrusts a Sister, and takes steps to open her barriers. By reaching out, she disperses walls and misunderstandings before they become conflicts, and her good will wins her a friend. By the opening up of her negativity, the Superior Woman finds harmony.

Six in the third line:
   She barriers pain.
   No error.
The Superior Woman struggles in a thankless and draining situation. She barriers her openness for protection and survival, and her barriers are essentially wise. Her trust is reserved for her Sisters, for the lover and family who cherish and heal her. She disperses her pain in company with them, and opens where she is safe. In a threatening environment, there is no blame in remaining closed and protected. The Superior Woman opens how and when she may.

Six in the fourth place:
> She opens to her circle
> And is healed.

The Superior Woman enters a spirituality circle to heal and be healed. In the safety and security of this space, she learns to open herself to her Sisters and the universe. She disperses the walls that protect her in everyday disappointments. By opening and sharing, she gains trust in her circle, and her Sisters gain trust in her. The women who achieve this find healing and love.

Nine in the fifth position:
> Dispersion of obstacles.
> She opens.

When obstacles and barriers reach their peak, change comes, and the tree accepts nourishment through her roots. The Superior Woman learns to recognize a point of opening. By taking advantage of any break in conflict, she helps to change her to accord. Openness brings unity in matriarchy and is a catalyst for dissolving struggle.

Nine at the top:
> Walls to protect another.
> She opens with care.

The Superior Woman builds walls for her Sister; her intentions are good and she tries to protect. No woman can protect or open another, unless the other consents and participates. The Superior Woman teaches her Sister to barrier and disperse, but she cannot do these things for her. No woman affects her Sister's free will without her approval and consent.

60. CHIEH / LIMITS

Above: K'an — The Chalice, Water

Below: Tui — The Joyous Daughter, Lake

The lake is bounded by her banks and overflows when filled beyond her limits. All filling reaches a point where emptying begins. The hexagram shows two aspects of water meeting and overflowing, and sets limits for them, as the Superior Woman sets limits for her desires and actions. She recognizes the right times for doing things; times to wait and times to act. She recognizes the limits of her body and knows when to rest. In times of giving, the Superior Woman gives, and in times of receiving she receives. By connection to the Wheel of Life and the Goddess, she experiences bounds and boundlessness in moderation.

THE CENTER — Limits. Good Moderation.

> Limits and limitations.
> She proceeds in temperance
> Neither loose or strict.
> Good fortune.

The Superior Woman sets limits in her life, but does so with self-love. She does not ask more of herself or her body than is possible. In her successes and failures, she accepts herself, and learns her growth and bounds. From her Sisters as well, the Superior Woman accepts limits and abilities as they occur in each woman. She does not force what her Sisters cannot give, or give what her Sisters cannot accept and take.

REFLECTION

> The lake fills the chalice:
> Limits.
> The Superior Woman
> Lives within bounds.

Water flows unbounded but a lake has banks. The Superior Woman sets limits in her life, and makes good choices in her tastes and actions. Limitlessness is uncomfortable, and unlimited possibility is fearful and without destination. The Superior Woman chooses her boundaries and becomes limitless within them. She chooses wisely and gives herself space to grow without being overwhelmed. Aware of boundaries and natural change in the universe, the Superior Woman sets limits to become truly free.

MOVEMENT

Nine at the beginning:
> Unlimited frustrations.
> She waits.

A woman with high goals finds herself blocked by frustrations that have no bounds. Her progress is limited for now, and she waits. By pausing to observe her situation, she understands her limits and learns what to do. In this way, the Superior Woman gains strategy for her goals.

Nine in the second place:
> She does not limit
> Her times to act.

Water overflows a lake that exceeds her boundaries, and the water finds somewhere to go. The Superior Woman acts when her limits of waiting are fulfilled. If she refuses her time for action, anxiety and indecision result, openings are missed, and growth is lost. The Superior Woman takes control of her actions, and opens the boundaries of her fate.

Six in the third line:
> Limitlessness.
> Misfortune.

A woman who immerses herself in shallow intemperance, who sets no limits on her actions, experiences self-harm and loss. The Superior Woman learns from her errors, and takes responsibility for limits that come from within. By learning to set, accept and maintain boundaries, she gains in harmony and peace.

Six in the fourth position:
> Realistic limits.
> She grows.

Excessive limitations take excessive work to maintain, and are therefore incorrect. Boundaries that are consistent with the cosmic order are effortless and peaceful to live by, and are the limits the Superior Woman needs. By realistic boundaries and freedoms, the Superior Woman achieves growth and self-love.

Nine in the fifth line:
>   She limits only herself.
>   She receives more.

The Superior Woman sets limits on herself, but does not set limits on others. If she asks of her Sisters less than what she gives of herself, her Sisters respond and give more with her. Correct limitation is based on tact and compassion; by giving she receives without setting bounds.

Six at the top:
>   Harsh limitations.
>   She errs.

The Superior Woman respects her body and mind, and does not demand unreasonable limits. She eats and dresses properly for comfort and health, does not abuse chemicals, and gets enough rest. In caring for herself she cares for her Sisters, as her Sisters follow her example. Harsh limitations cause reversing reactions, and these are to be avoided. The Superior Woman chooses her limits, and applies them gently, consistently and well.

61. CHUNG FU / INNER TRUTH

Above: Sun — The Gentle Wind/Wood

Below: Tui — The Joyous Daughter, Lake

Wind raises waves on the surface of a lake, and air is visible by result. The wind is gentle, perceptive and patient, and the lake is joyous and free with her inner strength. The trigrams are a picture of certainty in self and in the Goddess, certainty in matriarchy and her women. These qualities are inner truth, an attribute and goal of the Spiritual Woman.

THE CENTER — Inner Truth. She Gains Herself and the Universe.

> Inner truth.
> The Spiritual Woman
> Gains empowerment.

When the Spiritual Woman grounds herself in the earth and universe and opens herself to all that lives, she awakens to inner truth. The woman who is connected and centered in the Wheel of Life, in the Goddess, heals and finds healing peace. She comes into empowerment, into light and decision from within; her life affirms her inner strength, and she accomplishes great things. The Spiritual Woman is part of the Goddess, of her Sisters and matriarchy, and part of the earth and the stars.

REFLECTION

> Wind above water:
> Inner truth.
> The Spiritual Woman
> Is connected and clear.

Wind enters and changes the surface of a lake, and the Spiritual Woman enters the mysteries of being. The more she understands, the deeper is her respect for all that lives. Her connectedness changes her relationships with her Sisters, with her family and lover, with her matriarchy, and adds to her confidence and self-worth. By her participation in the universe, her inner truth, she gains only positive results.

MOVEMENT

> *Nine at the beginning:*
> She learns independence
> And clarity.

Inner truth depends on knowledge and certainty from within: the woman who comes into inner power reflects empowerment in her actions. She chooses decisively and with clear independence; she listens to advice, but no Sister determines her life. The Spiritual Woman takes action by dignity and resoluteness. She respects her Sisters as she learns to respect herself.

Nine in the second position:
> Her thought-forms gain influence.
> Good thoughts are good fortunes.

Thoughts have form, color and presence on the astral plane, and the Spiritual Woman projects thought-forms that reflect her inner awareness. Her projections in turn attract to her like-minded women. When her thoughts are pure and good, she attracts the purity and goodness of others. In doing so, her own inner being is magnified and reinforced, and her inner truth exerts influence on the world.

Six in the third line:
> She lives in her lover.
> Misfortune.

The Spiritual Woman does not live for her lover, nor submerge her own personality in their relationship. Lovers make a life together that is rooted in both their lives, in the sharing of their love, uniqueness and separate strengths. Two women who are strongly individual, who each thinks for herself, and who participates in her own life's choices and needs, have the inner truth to share their lives well.

Six in the fourth place:
> She follows inner truth.
> Clear goals.

The Spiritual Woman gains light from within, and illuminates her paths. By following the inner truth and integrity that connects her to the earth and universe, she understands the meaning of her goals. Remaining connected and grounded, the Spiritual Woman sees them through.

Nine in the fifth position:
> Truths connect.
> No error.

The Spiritual Woman receives what she asks for in measure of her inner truth. "The world consists of more than the physical reality. Magic does not work against nature . . . "* By understanding herself, the Spiritual Woman changes herself and her world in harmony. Through her thought-forms, deeds and choices, through her will and affirmation, the Spiritual Woman directs her life by inner truth.

---

*Diane Mariechild, *Mother Wit: A Feminist Guide to Psychic Development*, (Trumansburg, NY, The Crossing Press, 1981), p. 126.

Nine at the top:
    Empty words.
    She errs.

Empty words without inner truth and action are errors that accomplish nothing. The Spiritual Woman takes her being from within, and her outer life mirrors her inner self. The woman who glows serenely with peace and beauty, who radiates feeling, integrity and openness, brings these things from outside. The Spiritual Woman in her inner truth, does good in all she attempts.

62. HSIAO KUO / CONTINUING

Above: Chên — The Awakening, Thunder

Below: Kên — Keeping Still, Mountain

Preponderance of the Small is the Chinese name for this hexagram, called *Continuing* in *The Kwan Yin Book of Changes.* Strength in the inner trigram lines continues and wins against all obstacles and frustrations. The Superior Woman is equal to tasks of whatever difficulty by her confidence and continuing: in the challenges she faces, she does not give up. An amazon, warrior and survivor, her correctness achieves and prevails.

THE CENTER — Continuing. She Achieves her Goals.

    Continuing in all things.
    Achievement in time.
    The Superior Woman triumphs.

Strength, enduring and integrity combine for success, and these qualities come from within. They grow from connection to the spiral and the harmonies of the universal Wheel. The Superior Woman takes step by step actions towards her goals, and her triumphs in small things accumulate to great achievements. She continues through obstacles and adversity but does not engage in conflict. In times of prosperity, she is temperate and shares with her Sisters. The Superior Woman learns to reach and be free. Her nature is strong in courage, and in continuing she earns her dreams.

REFLECTION

> Awakening the mountain:
> Continuing.
> The Superior Woman
> Fulfills her goals.

A mountain storm is close and immanent, and the Superior Woman takes her attitude from the storm's awakening. She sets her goals clearly and achieves them by continuing in correctness. She lives a life of thought, spirituality and action, and takes control of her destiny by assuming responsibility for her deeds. Her feelings are open and her actions come from her feelings; her thoughts are based on integrity and thoughts and feelings combine. The Superior Woman lives a simple life, without arrogance or excess. She is one' with her Sisters, a power for good in her matriarchy, and shows caring and respect for her lover and Daughters. In her correct continuing, the Superior Woman is the mountain and the sky.

MOVEMENT

> *Six at the beginning:*
> Not yet ready,
> She waits.

The Superior Woman does not take on actions and tasks beyond her stage of growth. She waits in her time of waiting, and asks for help from her Mothers and Sisters in need. Continuing beyond reason or possibility of success is unwise. She does not fly against the storm, but waits for sun.

> *Six in the second line:*
> She seeks a Mother.
> Good outcome.

The Superior Woman meets a challenge new to her understanding and experience. Rather than attempt the situation with skills she is unable to control, she approaches a Mother for assistance and advice. By joining powers with a Sister stronger than herself, the Superior Woman learns new skills and strengthens her abilities. She reaches her goal by continuing in correctness, and her caution brings her good outcome.

Nine in the third place:
    She is confident and wise.
    She wins.
Care is needed, but too often is ignored. The Superior Woman acts from empowerment and strength, but blocks come for which she is not ready. Caution avoids many hindrances and errors. The Superior Woman combines confidence with wisdom in her need to continue and take charge. In doing so, she wins.

Nine in the fourth line:
    She takes care
    And holds back.
Strength is tempered by gentleness in the Superior Woman. She knows when to wait and continue. In this line, great care is called for; she takes no present action, but waits for better times. The Superior Woman learns patience and awareness from within. She does not force a situation that cannot be forced. To continue brings outward error, but waiting she holds on.

Six in the fifth position:
    They continue together.
    Matriarchy grows.
The Superior Woman works with her Sisters to lead and direct the matriarchy. Continuing together creates prosperity, accord and greatness for all. Matriarchy is made of the skills of all her Sisters; they further and achieve her goals.

Six at the top:
    She reaches wisely
    And continues well.
The Superior Woman aims for unrealistic heights. She does not win, and continuing brings her frustrations. A strong woman's reach

exceeds her grasp, and her grasp stretches as she continues in reaching. There is a point, however, where excess occurs, and not knowing where to stop is a disharmony with the earth and universe. The Superior Woman attracts no blame by her high ideals; when her goals are correct and in harmony with the life force she attains them. When they are not, she meets with error until she learns balance.

63. CHI CHI / TURNING THE WHEEL (COMPLETIONS)

```
___ ___
_____
___ ___
```

Above: K'an — The Chalice, Water

```
_____
___ ___
_____
```

Below: Li — The Wand, Fire

Chi Chi is related to Hexagram 11, *Peace.* She is a moment of pause and completion after return to universal harmony. The time is the fall equinox, September 22, the transition between summer and winter and the cusp between Virgo and Libra. At the equinox, day and night are of equal length in a moment of balance, an instant of perfect stillness before winter descends. Though this is a time of harvest and abundance, the year is waning and the earth prepares for death. Women of wicca meet to speak the Kore Chant, remembering that the seeds of fall become the new growth of spring. Hopi women enter the Kivas for ceremonies of healing and rebirth. This is the time of fulfillment, a time for thought and awareness, spirituality and clarity, integrity, inner truth and continuing. She is the time to turn the Wheel.

When balance is reached, change follows. Completions are positive, but are preludes to new beginnings and new cycles. *The Kwan Yin Book of Changes* reflects the Wheel of Life; like the cycle of seasons, the Wheel of the Year, she is ever changing. Each hexagram reflects the aspects of a moment, but the moments constantly change. The Wheel begins: she waxes, reaches balance, and she wanes to begin

again. She mirrors the Mysteries of the Goddess.

THE CENTER — Endings and Beginnings. The Wheel of Change.

> Turning the Wheel.
> Completions
> And continuing.
> She changes.

At a moment of completion change is already made. Success is gained and her realization is all. An instant of perfection occurs, of peace and balance, a moment of pause and harmony. By her judgment, choices, awareness and actions, the Spiritual Woman causes this moment to happen and remains alert in her change. Though all things are balanced, the new arises and proceeds from the old, and the future begins in the past. The Spiritual Woman exerts great care to make the most of her changing potential. She sets her future into motion at completion of her past.

REFLECTION

> The wand and chalice:
> Completions.
> The Spiritual Woman
> Turns the Wheel.

The chalice of source is beyond the wand of the life force, water over fire. Life flows away from earth, and Demeter's fires reap grain before withdrawing into death. Energy and power, the wand and chalice life force, are greatest when held in balance. There are moments of perfection in life, when all appears to be ordered and in control. Such times are poised to precede danger, and the Spiritual Woman recognizes them as temporary. Every completion is an ending and a new beginning.

MOVEMENT

> *Nine at the beginning:*
> She rushes completions.
> No error.

Activities move forward in a time of change, and move towards their goals. The Spiritual Woman sees completion in reach and rushes out to meet her. Force and haste are unwise, however, and the Spiritual Woman does not run uncontrolled. Her integrity and correctness are strong, and she makes no errors.

Six in the second line:
> She waits for completions.
> Good fortune.

Before completion, the Spiritual Woman finds a space where she cannot act. Her decisions are made and actions taken, and her plans are set in motion. The climax approaches, and she has no more to do. The Spiritual Woman waits calmly and remains strong and clear. She enters completion knowing that the time is soon.

Nine in the third place:
> Growth beyond completion.
> She fills.

After completion comes a time of growth. As water in a cup, the Spiritual Woman rises to fill, then empties to fill again. In the Wheel of the Year, fall follows summer and winter follows fall; rebirth comes at spring in turn. In matriarchy too, a time of completion and emptying of energies is followed by refilling and new projects. The Spiritual Woman takes rest at endings, rebuilds her powers for times to rebegin.

Six in the fourth position:
> Conflicts are met
> And completed.

In times of growth, small conflicts and errors are ignored. At completion with her changes, however, these obstacles return with greater meaning. The Spiritual Woman faces and resolves each error that arises. Conflicts left untended threaten balance, and stress her to tangents best avoided. When errors are met with and fully resolved, they are completed and cause no more damage.

Nine in the fifth place:
> Spirituality.
> Bright completions.

At completion, the Spiritual Woman realizes she has turned the

Wheel. She approaches her situation in connectedness to the Goddess and the spiral of the universe. By her awareness and inner development, she acts correctly and in balance with all life.

> *Six at the top:*
>   She looks forward
>   To completions.

The Spiritual Woman neither stops with good fortune nor gives up with failure and adversity. In the start that follows the turning of the Wheel, she rebegins. She learns from her errors and triumphs, and continues wiser in new cycles. The Spiritual Woman, in harmony with the Wheel of Life, progresses through winter towards spring.

64. WEI CHI / TURNING THE WHEEL (BEGINNINGS)

Above: Li — The Wand, Fire

Below: K'an — The Chalice, Water

The world awaits change, but change is not yet made to new beginnings. *Wei Chi* is a time of movement and anticipation, of hope and preparation for fulfillment. The trigram figures are opposites to each other, and fire and water are principle elements of the universe. Fire rising over water at sunrise is an awesome and beautiful sight.

Beginnings are represented in the Wheel of the Year by springtime, the season of changes between winter and summer. She is green, abundant and fertile, Aries in the zodiac and spring equinox in the wiccan and Hopi calendars. Day and night are of equal length, as in Hexagram 63, *Completions*, but this is a time of waxing instead of waning, a movement towards instead of beyond growth. This is the final hexagram of *The Kwan Yin Book of Changes*. The book opens with the universe and the earth (*Ch'ien* and *K'un*) and ends with completions and beginnings. The Wheel of Life comes round once more: the circle is open but unbroken, blessed be.

THE CENTER — After Completions, Beginnings.

> After completions, beginnings.
> After beginnings, completions.
> The Wheel continues and turns.

The Chinese title for this hexagram is *Before Completion*, and for Hexagram 63, *After Completion*. Both are beginnings, but are dualities and opposites. After completions come new starts, and beginnings proceed to new ends. All contradictions and opposites are one in the mirror, in the turnings of the Wheel of Life; the circle is an endless ring, without start or stop. Beginnings are tenuous times and the task is enormous, but possibilities are unlimited in potential. The Spiritual Woman works towards her best good fortune, and she and her matriarchy triumph. In beginnings and completions she fulfills her Wheel.

REFLECTION

> The chalice and wand:
> Beginnings.
> Order and peace
> In her progress.

The fire of life reaches upward and water cups down in her depths. Seeming contradictions, each exists in her place. The Spiritual Woman centers her life in the balance of cosmic order, where all dualities are one. With enlightenment, care and clarity, she moves towards harmony and peace. Her beginnings approach completions and fulfillments, and the turning Wheel revolves to new hope.

MOVEMENT

> *Six at the beginning:*
> Beginnings in their times.
> No error.

At the beginning of change, the Spiritual Woman rushes into

action. She wants peace and fulfillment as quickly as possible. If the beginning is incorrect, however, forcing her leads to disappointment and loss. The Spiritual Woman, while keeping her goals in sight and her integrity strong, knows when to wait and to start.

Nine in the second position:
     Early beginnings.
     She waits.
The Spiritual Woman waits for her opportunity and gains the courage to continue and achieve. She develops skills needed to attain her desires, and learns connectedness to the universe and the Goddess. The time she waits is not wasted, but prepares her to act and begin.

Six in the third line:
     Beginnings become
     Completions.
Beginnings become completions through change, and change is the nature of the Wheel of Life. In a time of subtle or great transformation, the Spiritual Woman takes charge of her fate. Though change is natural and inevitable, she controls and influences her. With energy, decision and awareness, the Spiritual Woman affects beginnings and moves them towards resolutions.

Nine in the fourth place:
     Adversity, doubt and conflict.
     She endures to begin.
Changes are brought to completions and new beginnings, but the meantime is conflict and doubt. The Spiritual Woman trades obstacles for choice and rejects negativity and fear. By her connectedness and correctness, she acts well, and proceeds to new beginnings as completions are made. Continuing brings her achievement, balance and peace.

Six in the fifth position:
     She gains beginnings.
     Bright achievement.
The Spiritual Woman, through light and perseverance, gains her goal. She shines in strength and integrity, and her beginnings are ended and fulfilled. The Spiritual Woman's completions and beginnings arrive by resolution, with prosperity, success and hope.

Nine at the top:
>   They begin in circle
>   And celebrate.

In beginnings, when the old is ended and the new is a bright potential, women of matriarchy join together in a circle. They draw down the Moon and speak the Kore Chant of spring's rebirth. Perfect love and perfect trust are raised with power in their rituals; the Sisters are in harmony with the earth and the stars. At one with each other, with the Wheel of Life and the Goddess, they celebrate peace.

THE WHEEL OF THE YEAR

Chinese Month	Zodiac Sign	Sabbats	Hexagrams
First Month February-March	Capricorn and Aquarius 12/22 - 2/19	Chinese New Year Brigid/Candlemas Powamu	11 - Peace
Second Month March-April	Pisces and Pisces 2/19 - 4/20	Spring Equinox Eostar Isumúya and Kwiyamúya	34 - Justice 64 - Beginnings
Third Month April-May	Aries and Taurus 3/20 - 5/21	Spring Beltane Kwiyamúya	42 - Resolution
Fourth Month May-June	Taurus and Gemini 4/20 - 6/21	Beltane Úimúya	43 - Letting Go
Fifth Month June-July	Gemini and Cancer 5/21 - 7/23	Summer Solstice Litha/ Midsummer's Night Kamuya & Kelmuya	14-TheGoddess' Gifts 44 - Coming to Meet
Sixth Month July-August	Cancer and Leo 6/21 - 8/23	Late Summer Lammas Pámuya (2nd)	30 - Caressing Fire
Seventh Month August- September	Leo and Virgo 7/23 - 9/23	Lammas Flute and Snake Antelope Ceremonies	12 - Disharmony 33 - Withdrawal

Chinese Month	Zodiac Sign	Sabbats	Hexagrams
Eighth Month September- October	Virgo and Libra 8/23 - 10/23	Fall Equinox Mabon or Mab Eusaumúya	55 - Abundance 63 - Completions
Ninth Month October- November	Scorpio 10/23 - 11/23	Samhain/Hallows Wuwúchim	23 - Splitting Apart
Tenth Month November - December	Scorpio & Sagittarius 10/23 - 12/22	Late Fall — Samhain to Yule	20 - Contempla- tion
Eleventh Month December - January	Capricorn 12/22 - 1/19	Winter Solstice Yule Soyál	24 - Wheel of Life
Twelfth Month January - February	Capricorn and Aquarius 12/22 - 2/19	Chinese New Year Brigid/Candlemas Pámuya	19 - Approach

THE ZODIAC YEAR

March 21 - April 20	—	Aries
April 21 - May 21	—	Taurus
May 22 - June 21	—	Gemini
June 22 - July 23	—	Cancer
July 24 - August 23	—	Leo
August 24 - September 23	—	Virgo
September 24 - October 23	—	Libra
October 24 - November 22	—	Scorpio
November 23 - December 22	—	Sagittarius
December 23 - January 20	—	Capricorn
January 21 - February 18	—	Aquarius
February 19 - March 20	—	Pisces

THE HOPI ROAD OF LIFE*

English Month	English Reference	Hopi Month	Hopi Ceremony/s
December	Winter Solstice The return and Acceptance of the Road	Kamuya (Respected Moon)	Soyál The Kachinas' Return to the Pueblos
January	Period between Soyal and Powamu	Pámuya (Moisture Moon)	Kachina Night Dances
February	Purification and Initiation of the Road of Life	Powámúya	Powamu (The sprouted beans in the kivas)
March	Spring Equinox Preparations for Planting	Isumúya (March, Whispering Noises of Breezes); Kwiyamúya (April, Windbreaker); Uimúya (May, The Planting Moon)	Kachina Night Dances Ladder Dance No major ceremonials
July	Summer Solstice The Leaving of the Kachinas	Second Kélemuya Month (Hawk or Initiates Moon)	Niman Kachina Home Dances Spruce Tree Ceremony
August	The Great Marriage (Bi-yearly)	Second Pámuya Month (Moisture Moon)	Flute Ceremony Green Corn Dances Snake-Antelope Ceremony (bi-yearly)

*Frank Waters, *Book of the Hopi*, (New York, Ballantine Books, 1963), p. 168-292.

English Month	English Reference	Hopi Month	Hopi Ceremony/s
September-October	Fall Equinox Women's Healing Ceremonies	Eusaumuya	Lakón Márawu Owaq̈lt
November	The New Year The Emergence	Kélemuya (Hawk or Initiates Moon)	Wúwuchim

THE WICCAN CALENDAR

December 22	—	Winter Solstice, Yule
February 2	—	Brigid, Candlemas, or Imbolc
March 21	—	Spring Equinox, Eostar
May 1	—	Beltane or May Eve
June 22	—	Summer Solstice, Midsummer's Night or Litha
August 1	—	Lammas, Lughnassad or The Green Corn Festival
September 22	—	Fall Equinox, Mabon
October 31	—	Samhain, Hallows or Hallowmas, The New Year

APPENDIX II
TAROT CORRESPONDENCES

All correspondences are based on the Motherpeace Tarot system of Vicki Noble and Karen Vogel in *Motherpeace: A Way to the Goddess Through Myth, Art and Tarot,* (San Francisco, Harper and Row Publishers, 1983).

1.	Ch'ien - The Creative Universe	Ace of Swords
2.	K'un - The Receptive Earth	The Empress
3.	Chun - Beginnings	Ace of Wands
4.	Mêng - Youthful Folly	The Fool
5.	Hsŭ - Waiting Nourishment	Four of Cups
6.	Sung - Conflict	Seven of Swords
7.	Shih - The Women	Judgment
8.	Pi - Holding Together (Union)	Lovers
9.	Hsiao Ch'u - The Cleansing Wind	Shaman of Swords
10.	Lŭ - Treading Softly (Correctness)	Daughter of Swords
11.	T'ai - Peace	Strength
12.	P'i - Disharmony (Waning)	Death
13.	T'ung Jên - Sisterhood	Two of Wands
14.	Ta Yu - The Goddess' Gifts	Six of Wands
15.	Ch'ien - Temperance	Temperance
16.	Yŭ - Enthusiasm (Willingness)	Three of Discs
17.	Sui - Following	Eight of Cups
18.	Ku - Decay	The Hierophant
19.	Lin - Approach	Ace of Disks
20.	Kuan - Contemplation (Example)	Priestess of Swords
21.	Shih Ho - Taking Hold (Recourse)	Five of Wands
22.	Pi - Grace	Eight of Discs
23.	Po - Splitting Apart	The Tower
24.	Fu - The Wheel of Life (Return)	Wheel of Fortune
25.	Wu Wang - Innocence (Wonder)	Daughter of Discs
26.	Ta Ch'u - The Wisewoman (Grounding)	The Crone
27.	I - Providing Nourishment (Caring)	Six of Discs
28.	Ta Kuo - Interesting Times	The Emperor
29.	K'an - The Depths	High Priestess
30.	Li - The Caressing Fire	The Sun

PART II

31.	Hsien - Influence (Courtship)	Two of Cups
32.	Hêng - Duration (Lovers)	The Chariot
33.	Tun - Withdrawal	Four of Swords
34.	Ta Chuang - Justice	Shaman of Wands
35.	Chin - Success	The Magician
36.	Ming I - Adversity	Nine of Wands
37.	Chia Jên - The Matriarchy	The World
38.	K'uei - Opposition	Seven of Wands
39.	Chien - Obstruction	Seven of Discs
40.	Hsieh - Release	Ten of Cups
41.	Sun - Restraint (Lessening)	Daughter of Cups
42.	Kuai - Resolution (Progress)	Three of Swords
43.	I - Letting Go (Gaining)	Daughter of Wands
44.	Kou - Coming to Meet	Six of Swords
45.	Ts'ui - Gathering Together	Ten of Discs
46.	Shêng - The Tree of Life (Reaching)	Priestess of Discs
47.	K'un - Depletion	Five of Cups
48.	Ching - The Well	Nine of Cups
49.	Ko - Change and Transformations	Hanged One
50.	Ting - The Cauldron	Shaman of Cups
51.	Chên - Awakening	Four of Wands
52.	Kên - Centering (Connecting)	Nine of Discs
53.	Chien - Development (Growth)	Shaman of Discs
54.	Kuei Mei - Living Together	Three of Cups
55.	Fêng - Abundance (Fullness)	Justice
56.	Lü - The Wanderer	Eight of Wands
57.	Sun - The Gentle	Two of Swords
58.	Tui - Joy	Ace of Cups
59.	Huan - Opening (Dispersion)	Ten of Swords
60.	Chieh - Limits	Seven of Cups
61.	Chung Fu - Inner Truth	Priestess of Cups
62.	Hsiao Kuo - Continuing	Priestess of Wands
63.	Chi Chi - Turning the Wheel (Completions)	The Moon
64.	Wei Chi - Turning the Wheel (Beginnings)	The Star

There are seventy-eight cards in the Tarot and sixty-four hexagrams in the *I Ching*. Fourteen Tarot cards are therefore undesignated.

THE MAJOR ARCANA

0 - The Fool	4. Mêng - Youthful Folly
1 - The Magician	35. Chin - Success
2 - High Priestess	29. K'an - The Depths
3 - The Empress	2. K'un - The Receptive Earth
4 - The Emperor	28. Ta Kuo - Interesting Times
5 - The Hierophant	18. Ku - Decay
6 - Lovers	8. Pi - Holding Together (Union)
7 - The Chariot	32. Hêng - Duration (Lovers)
8 - Justice	55. Fêng - Abundance (Fullness)
9 - The Crone	26. Ta Ch'u - The Wisewoman (Grounding)
10 - Wheel of Fortune	24. Fu - The Wheel of Life (return)
11 - Strength	11. T'ai - Peace
12 - Hanged One	49. Ko - Change and Transformations
13 - Death	12. P'i - Disharmony (Waning)
14 - Temperance	15. Ch'ien - Temperance
15 - The Devil	- - - - - - - - -
16 - The Tower	23. Po - Splitting Apart
17 - The Star	64. Wei Chi - Turning the Wheel (Beginnings)
18 - The Moon	63. Chi Chi - Turning the Wheel (Completions)
19 - The Sun	30. Li - The Caressing Fire
20 - Judgment	7. Shih - The Women
21 - The World	37. Chia Jên - The Matriarchy

THE MINOR ARCANA
Swords (Air)

Ace	1. Ch'ien - The Creative Universe
Two	57. Sun - The Gentle
Three	42. Kuai - Resolution (Progress)
Four	33. Tun - Withdrawal
Five	--------
Six	44. Kou - Coming to Meet
Seven	6. Sung - Conflict
Eight	---------
Nine	---------
Ten	59. Huan - Opening (Dispersion)
Daughter	10. Lü - Treading Softly (Correctness)
Son	---------
Priestess	20. Kuan - Contemplation (Example)
Shaman	9. Hsiao Ch'u - The Cleansing Wind

THE MINOR ARCANA
Wands (Fire)

Ace	3. Chun - Beginnings
Two	13. T'ung Jên - Sisterhood
Three	---------
Four	51. Chên - Awakening
Five	21. Shih Ho - Taking Hold (Recourse)
Six	14. Ta Yu - The Goddess' Gifts
Seven	38. K'eui - Opposition
Eight	56. Lü - The Wanderer
Nine	36. Ming I - Adversity
Ten	---------
Daughter	43. I - Letting Go (Gaining)
Son	---------
Priestess	62. Hsiao Kuo - Continuing
Shaman	34. Ta Chuang - Justice

THE MINOR ARCANA
Cups (Water)

Ace	58. Tui - Joy
Two	31. Hsien - Influence (Courtship)
Three	54. Kuei Mei - Living Together
Four	5. Hsü - Waiting Nourishment
Five	47. K'un - Depletion
Six	- - - - - - - - -
Seven	60. Chieh - Limits
Eight	17. Sui - Following
Nine	48. Ching - The Well
Ten	40. Hsieh - Release
Daughter	41. Sun - Restraint (Lessening)
Son	- - - - - - - - -
Priestess	61. Chung Fu - Inner Truth
Shaman	50. Ting - The Cauldron

THE MINOR ARCANA
Discs (Earth)

Ace	19. Lin - Approach
Two	- - - - - - - - -
Three	16. Yü - Enthusiasm (Willingness)
Four	- - - - - - - - -
Five	- - - - - - - - -
Six	27. I - Providing Nourishment (Caring)
Seven	39. Chien - Obstruction
Eight	22. Pi - Grace
Nine	52. Kên - Centering (Connecting)
Ten	45. Ts'ui - Gathering Together
Daughter	25. Wu Wang - Innocence (Wonder)
Son	- - - - - - - - -
Priestess	46. Shêng - The Tree of Life (Reaching)
Shaman	53. Chien - Development (Growth)

BIBLIOGRAPHY

Fairfield, Gail, *Choice Centered Tarot*, (Seattle, Choice Centered Astrology and Tarot, 1982).

Mariechild, Diane, *Mother Wit: A Feminist Guide to Psychic Development*, (Trumansburg, New York, The Crossing Press, 1981).

Noble, Vicki, *Motherpeace: A Way to the Goddess Through Myth, Art and Tarot*, (San Francisco, Harper and Row Publishers, 1983).

Starhawk, *The Spiral Dance: A Rebirth of the Ancient Religion of the Great Goddess*, (San Francisco, Harper and Row Publishers, 1979).
  Dreaming the Dark: Magic, Sex and Politics, (Boston, Beacon Press, 1982).

Thorsten, Geraldine, *God Herself: The Feminine Roots of Astrology*, (New York, Avon Books, 1980).

Waters, Frank, *Book of the Hopi*, (New York, Ballantine Books, 1963).

Weinstein, Marion, *Earth Magic: A Dianic Book of Shadows*, (Custer, Washington, Phoenix Publishing Company, 1980).

Wilhelm, Richard and Cary F. Baynes, Trans., *The I Ching or Book of Changes*, Bollingen Series XIX, (Princeton, Princeton University Press, 1950 and 1967).

Notes about KWAN YIN

Among the Chinese farming community, the Goddess of Mercy is invoked, especially in time of trouble.

In the normal practice, a man approaches the Goddess through a woman intermediary; this may be his wife or some other member of the household. Should no woman be available, then the man may himself go: in such case, having first apologized for the omission, he gives an offering to the priestess of the Goddess.

She was either represented standing, or, more often, seated on a rock island in the Indian Ocean, dressed in splendid garments *or* jewelry . . . She is quite commonly bare-footed. She is also frequently depicted with an incense burner or a pot in Her right hand; and with Her left hand holding up Her flowing robe.

She is the Goddess who hears the cry of the world and lays aside Her Buddhahood for the sake of the suffering world. She is the Great Mother in her character of loving Sophia.

In *The Secret Doctrine*, Kwan Yin is closely associated with sound. She is here described as a manifestation of the occult potency of sound in Aethyr and Nature; She is called "the melodious Voice" and is connected with the force, *Fohat*.

As a giver of oracles, Kwan Yin appears in the sagas connected with the magician *Aunt Piety*.

Kwan Yin is also a magician and teacher of magic.

The Festival of Kwan Yin is celebrated April 5th.

(Above all taken from *The Goddesses of India, Tibet, China and Japan* by Lawrence Durdin-Robertson, Cesara Publications, Eire, 1976.)

From the same book, page 211, in reference to Kundalini . . .

Every woman . . . is the begetter of more than bodies.

THE CHARGE OF THE GODDESS*

I who am the beauty of the green earth and the white moon among the stars and the mysteries of the waters, I call upon your soul to arise and come unto me. For I am the soul of nature that gives life to the universe. From Me all things proceed and unto Me they must return. Let My worship be in the heart that rejoices, for behold — all acts of love and pleasure are My rituals. Let there be beauty and strength, power and compassion, honor and humility, mirth and reverence within you. And you who seek to know Me, know that your seeking and yearning will avail you not, unless you know the Mystery: for if that which you seek, you find not within yourself, you will never find it without. For behold, I have been with you from the beginning, and I am that which is attained at the end of desire.

Traditional

*Quoted in: Starhawk, *The Spiral Dance: The Rebirth of the Ancient Religion of the Great Goddess*, (San Francisco, Harper and Row Publishers, 1979), p. 76.

STAY IN TOUCH

On the following pages you will find listed, with their current prices, some of the books now available on related subjects. Your book dealer stocks most of these and will stock new titles in the Llewellyn series as they become available. We urge your patronage.

To obtain our full catalog, to keep informed about new titles as they are released and to benefit from informative articles and helpful news, you are invited to write for our bimonthly news magazine/catalog, *Llewellyn's New Worlds of Mind and Spirit*. A sample copy is free, and it will continue coming to you at no cost as long as you are an active mail customer. Or you may subscribe for just $7.00 in the U.S.A. and Canada ($20.00 overseas, first class mail). Many bookstores also have *New Worlds* available to their customers. Ask for it.

Stay in touch! In *New Worlds'* pages you will find news and features about new books, tapes and services, announcements of meetings and seminars, articles helpful to our readers, news of authors, products and services, special money-making opportunities, and much more.

Llewellyn's New Worlds of Mind and Spirit
P.O. Box 64383-760, St. Paul, MN 55164-0383, U.S.A.
* * *

TO ORDER BOOKS AND TAPES

If your book dealer does not have the books described on the following pages readily available, you may order them directly from the publisher by sending full price in U.S. funds, plus $3.00 for postage and handling for orders *under* $10.00; $4.00 for orders *over* $10.00. There are no postage and handling charges for orders over $50.00. Postage and handling rates are subject to change. UPS Delivery: We ship UPS whenever possible. Delivery guaranteed. Provide your street address as UPS does not deliver to P.O. Boxes. UPS to Canada requires a $50.00 minimum order. Allow 4-6 weeks for delivery. Orders outside the U.S.A. and Canada: Airmail—add retail price of book; add $5.00 for each non-book item (tapes, etc.); add $1.00 per item for surface mail.

FOR GROUP STUDY AND PURCHASE

Because there is a great deal of interest in group discussion and study of the subject matter of this book, we feel that we should encourage the adoption and use of this particular book by such groups by offering a special quantity price to group leaders or agents.

Our special quantity price for a minimum order of five copies of *The Kwan Yin Book of Changes* is $29.85 cash-with-order. This price includes postage and handling within the United States. Minnesota residents must add 6.5% sales tax. For additional quantities, please order in multiples of five. For Canadian and foreign orders, add postage and handling charges as above. Credit card (VISA, Master-Card, American Express) orders are accepted. Charge card orders only ($15.00 minimum order) may be phoned in free within the U.S.A. or Canada by dialing 1-800-THE-MOON. For customer service, call 1-612-291-1970. Mail orders to:

LLEWELLYN PUBLICATIONS
P.O. Box 64383-760, St. Paul, MN 55164-0383, U.S.A.

THE WOMEN'S SPIRITUALITY BOOK
by Diane Stein

Here is a work of insight and a much needed addition to women's magic and ritual. Beginning with "Creation and Creation Goddesses" Diane Stein enthusiastically informs the reader of the essence of women-centered Wicca, using myths and legends drawn from a variety of world sources to bring her work to life. Nonpatriarchal myths and tales intersperse the first half of the book, which leads the reader through the yearly progressions of rituals in some of the most complete descriptions of the Sabbats ever published.

The second half of the book is a valuable introduction to visualization, healing, chakras, crystal and gemstone magick. Subsequent chapters cover "transformational tarot" and Kwan Yin.

The Women's Spirituality Book is a tool for self-discovery and initiation into the Higher Self: a joyous reunion with the Goddess.
0-87542-761-8, 288 pgs., 6 x 9, illus., softcover **$9.95**

THE WOMEN'S BOOK OF HEALING
by Diane Stein

At the front of the women's spirituality movement with her previous books, Diane Stein now helps women (and men) reclaim their natural right to be healers. Included are exercises which can help YOU to become a healer! Learn about the uses of color, vibration, crystals and gems for healing. Learn about the auric energy field and the chakras.

The book teaches alternative healing theory and techniques and combines them with crystal and gemstone healing, laying on of stones, psychic healing, laying on of hands, chakra work and aura work, and color therapy. It teaches beginning theory in the aura, chakras, colors, creative visualization, meditation, health theory and ethics with some quantum theory. Forty-six gemstones plus clear quartz crystals are discussed in detail, arranged by chakras and colors.

The Women's Book of Healing is a book designed to teach basic healing (Part I) and healing with crystals and gemstones (Part II). Part I discusses the aura and four bodies; the chakras; basic healing skills of creative visualization, meditation and color work; psychic healing; and laying on of hands. Part II begins with a chapter on clear quartz crystal, then enters gemstone work with introductory gemstone material. The remainder of the book discusses, in chakra-by-chakra format, specific gemstones for healing work, their properties and uses.
0-87542-759-6, 352 pgs., 6 x 9, illus., softcover **$12.95**

STROKING THE PYTHON
Women's Psychic Lives
by Diane Stein
This book is a comprehensive course in psychic understanding, and ends women's psychic isolation forever. It contains the theory and explanation of psychic phenomena, women's shared and varied experiences, and how-to material for every woman's growth and psychic development. The reclamation of being psychic is women's reclamation of Goddess—and of their Goddess Being.

That reclaiming of women's psychic abilities and psychic lives is a major issue in Goddess spirituality and in the wholeness of women. Learning that everyone is psychic, learning what the phenomena mean, sharing and understanding others' experiences, and learning how to develop women's own abilities is information women are ready and waiting for in this dawning Age of Aquarius and Age of Women.

In the Greek legends of Troy, Cassandra, daughter of Hecuba, was gifted with prophecy. She gained her gift as a child at Delphi when she Stroked the Pythons of Gaea's temple, becoming a psychic priestess. Gaea, the Python, was the Goddess of oracles and mother/creator of the Earth.

In this book are fascinating accounts of women's psychic experiences. Learn how to develop your own, natural psychic abilities through the extensive advice given in *Stroking the Python.*
0-87542-757-X, 381 pgs., 6 x 9, illus., softcover   **$12.95**

RECLAIMING WOMAN'S VOICE
Becoming Whole
by Lesley Shore, Ph.D.
Many of today's difficulties stem from a fundamental imbalance in the core of our world. We have lost our ties with mother Earth and the feminine in our nature. The feminine is suppressed, oppressed —abused. And while everyone suffers the consequences of society's devaluation of the feminine, this book primarily explores its effects on women.

Women's voice finds expression in psychological and psychosomatic symptoms. Many women are depressed or anxious. They are troubled by low self-esteem and suffer from eating disorders and other addictions. They question their beauty and their bodies.

This book shows women how to discover what their symptoms are telling them about their hidden needs and blocked energies. Once the cause of these symptom are found, women can then move on with their lives, become whole human beings, live in harmony with inner rhythms, and finally feel good about themselves.
0-87542-722-7, 208 pgs., 5-1/4 x 8 , softcover   **$9.95**

Prices subject to change without notice.